And Another Thing ...

Written by Don Wooten

Published by
Moline Dispatch Publishing Company, L.L.C.
1720 Fifth Avenue
Moline, IL 61265

Additional copies of this book can be ordered online at qconline.com/books.

ISBN: 978-0-9761162-9-5

Happy Anniversary Bernadette

Apologia

A funny thing happens to a number of over-the-hill guys: they decide to write books. Few such projects actually make it through publication, but collecting old notes and writing about the past helps geezers pass the time innocently, allows them to adjust old memories, settle scores, and, perhaps, convince their kids that they were at least semi-important.

Of course, I have a much nobler motive: recycling.

I have written over 1,100 columns for the Argus and Dispatch (only half that number have appeared in the latter newspaper) and they have been piling up in portfolios, folders, and files since 1986. I got to wondering what, if anything, could be made of them.

Some gifted writers (my personal favorite is Dave Barry) simply scoop up a year's worth of weekly essays and dump them on the market, to critical applause and financial gain. I realized that my scattershot approach to topics couldn't be dealt with the same way or to similar ends.

Still, there must be something in that mass of paper which bears repeating. Or amending. Or supplementing. Besides, re-cycling is a virtuous activity. And since retiring, I really haven't anything else to do.

So, let's see …

If You Have To Explain ...

I think I should.

What follows is an assortment of columns published in two Illinois newspapers, The Rock Island Argus and The Dispatch in Moline, between 1986 and the near-present. They follow no chronological order, but are grouped in small, semi-coherent bundles which center on a general topic. There really is no master plan here; I just followed instinct and caprice in deciding what material to use.

Here and there, I have done some re-writing; shortening and combining when it seemed appropriate, but left the bulk of them as I found them in the computer. In most cases, they are dated, which will help explain references to people and events which have passed from the public's six-month collective memory.

Of course, nothing would have appeared in book form without the generous consent of Len R. Small, owner of the Small Newspaper Group. He is also the man who talked me into writing columns in the first place, so he bears a heavy responsibility.

He also has my gratitude for permitting me to reprint most of the material within. I must also express my thanks to the editors who have dealt gently with my writing through the years. The most recent of them are Kenda Burrows and Murray Hancks. I am also grateful to Molly Clodius, who salvaged pre-computer columns for me. And a deep obeisance is due Sally Trulson and Sarah Nimrick for making a book out of it all.

Roald Tweet is another who has to answer for this. He encouraged me to write a book. But then, he encourages everyone to publish. He also had the patience to read much of the manuscript.

Bill Hannan, the Quad-Cities' universal artist, did the artwork, even as he has illustrated much of my work in television and theatre through the past fifty years. Bill is a generous man who has spent his life and talents doing like service for dozens of individuals and institutions in the Quad-Cities.

Finally, my heaviest debt is to my wife, Bernadette, who has read or listened to everything I have ever written, approving of it all. A living saint.

And Another Thing ...

Contents

Grinding It Out

Writers complain a lot. You'd think that assembling words on paper is onerous work, the kind of grinding toil one associates with highway construction or garbage-collecting.

It is.

(11 January 2004)

Before starting this project, I went digging through my files for my very first column, dated January 12, 1986, just to see what I had written. Here's the way it started, with a frighteningly honest statement:

Just what the world needs: another columnist.

I haven't seen any opinion polls on the subject, but I imagine that most readers would agree with Harold Ickes, who sized up the profession in 1939:

7

"The columnist's stock in trade is falsification and vilification. He is journalism's Public Enemy No. 1, and, if the American press is to improve itself, it must get rid of him."

Thank heavens standards haven't risen since those Depression Days and the tribe of columnists increases. And some of us grow old.

The bulk of that first essay was personal. I thought it proper to introduce myself to the reader, giving some family and career details and something of my state of mind. Looking it over now, I find that not much has changed.

On reflection, I guess it was an odd way to begin a newspaper assignment, but it's only natural to want to justify yourself to people who will know you only through the printed page.

No one likes to be misunderstood, but reading is as creative as writing and the words you use to convey a specific thought may well yield something contrary when read by a person of a different mindset.

That said, let me repeat a few things I wrote over 20 years ago. What follows won't fully explain the way my mind works, but it will give you a limited view from inside. If you want to read the original article, it's in The Argus archives. Here are some slightly amended excerpts:

I was born in Memphis, Tennessee, and came north to enter the seminary at St. Ambrose College in Davenport. I left the seminary after two years, but hung around afterward, working my way through college by working the switchboard at night and managing the Music Department by day.

My college training was in biology and education, with minors in Latin, philosophy, and music. So, I went into radio and television and have remained in the profession, except for an eight-year foray into politics (1972-1980) as Illinois State Senator (Democrat, 36th District).

On the side, I taught high school off and on for almost 20 years (Alleman High School, Rock Island, IL) and started a classical theatre group, the Genesius Guild, in 1956. I built public radio station WVIK for Augustana College in 1980 and have since retired from all of it. I talk a lot, write a little, and read whenever a good book is at hand.

I married Bernadette Polka in 1950 and we have five children: daughters in Denver (Cece), near Tacoma (Chris), and Anchorage (Teri); sons in Daytona Beach (Steve) and Rock Island (David).

I am wary of automobiles, great wealth, and power; three useful things which can corrupt and pollute. I am restless, rebellious, but deeply committed to avoiding quarrels. I am fiscally and personally conservative, but quite willing to use government to achieve any potentially useful or beneficial end.

Above all, for one who has lived all his adult years in public, I prefer privacy, even solitude. The contradiction is that I enjoy people, but often avoid most personal contact.

My behavior is orthodox, but my thoughts are heretical and I am hesitant to put those thoughts in writing. I usually do so in a quasi-humorous or even-handed manner to forestall readers' apoplexy.

I have also grown suspicious of orthodox religion. In fact, the religious impulse frightens me, as it often prompts otherwise decent people to burn witches, exclude non-believers, and become militantly self-righteous. Yet, I have a strong attachment to the Catholic Church, in spite of its monarchical structure and tendencies. I really believe in the impossible admonition: "Love your enemy; do good to those who hate you."

I admire great souls and have a special regard for those who work to improve things. This includes Pope John XXIII, Edward R. Murrow, Franklin D. Roosevelt, the O'Connor Brothers (Ambrosians know them), Arturo Toscanini, and dozens of others whose names have meaning only for me.

I hold in awe those friends and family members who have put up with me for these many years. It hasn't been easy for them and I wonder why they do it.

Like everyone else, I wonder why we are the way we are and what it all means. I think the world's overriding problem is that people tend to behave (the publisher hated this simile) like self-aware bacteria. Individually, we think, reason, and judge well enough. But in a group, we are drawn to ideologies, trends, charismatic leaders, and similar ephemera as some bacteria are drawn to light. This keeps us in thrall to the worst sort of politicians, entertainers, hucksters, and combinations of the three.

I am fairly confident that it will all work out, if we can get over the primitive tribal and nationalistic emotions which prompt us to tolerate policies we know to be self-destructive.

And I really hate to write anything, including this column. I keep going with the expectation that it will give me time off in purgatory.

(18 April 1999)

Yesterday, I spent some time leafing through a collection of my old columns. It wasn't a stroll down memory lane. I was in the final stage of desperation in choosing a topic for this Sunday. Unable to think of anything new, I thought I might be able be recycle something old.

My search turned up nothing useful, but it did trigger some old questions and thoughts about this job. When I was first asked to write for the Argus, it was not so much a request, as a gentle command. The new owner wanted a weekly feature by a Rock Island resident and picked me for the task.

Believe it or not, I turned the offer down. But that didn't end the conversation. As we continued to talk, he advanced a variety of plausible reasons for reconsidering my refusal. He capped it off with an appeal to friendship, so I reluctantly agreed to give it a try.

What clinched the deal was the owner's assurance that I could skip the column any time I wanted. (During the first year, I took advantage of that out no less than seven times.) Furthermore, I could quit for good whenever I chose.

There remained only one quibble: what should I write about? I never got a straight answer. When I pressed for some kind of guidance, he sent me an article on how to write a newspaper column.

Over the course of many subsequent conversations, when trying to narrow the focus of the column, I was counseled that "local subjects are best, but feel free to discuss anything at all." When I insisted on clearer instructions, I got another article on "How to Write about Anything in 750 Words or Less".

And so I have wandered all over the lot, swinging from heavy-handed analysis to something like free association. During the first few years I wrote a lot about politics, having been out of the Illinois legislature but a short time. I still dip into the subject, but now from the more remote and less closely-informed position of a private citizen.

One year I did a series of impassioned columns on racial issues, but I felt uncomfortably certain that few people read them all the way through. On the other hand, when I write silly stuff about weeding the yard or talking to my dog, I hear about it from readers for weeks.

Don't get me wrong: I am not buried under an avalanche of mail. Written response to these articles is sparse. But then, this is not a letter-writing age. I suspect that most readers either nod in agreement or toss the paper aside in anger and let it go at that. I am told phone comments are sometimes made to Speak Out, but I never take that seriously.

When I do get letters, I am struck by the divergent reactions they contain. No matter what position I take on any given topic, the positive and negative response to it is just about equally balanced. To be scrupulously truthful, I should mention that I receive (but never read) anonymous letters on occasion. I think it's fair to assign them to the negative pile.

If one may judge from the comments I pick up in casual conversation, most readers prefer lighter subjects. I certainly understand and sympathize with that attitude. After all, the only columnist I read every single week is Dave Barry. I like the outrageous Molly Ivins, the cerebral David Brooks, the judicious David Broder, and all the rest, but I never miss Barry.

So, if that's my preference, why should I expect others to tackle the double-domed, doom-saying stuff that thoughtful commentators serve up on everything from Kosovo to environmental degradation to the stock market and less respectable forms of gambling?

But, beyond the question of what to write about, there is the larger question of who should do the writing. There are a number of thoughtful people in this community whose ideas are worth general circulation, but they aren't in the newspaper every week.

I must add here that the editors do a pretty fair job of combing through the population looking for such writers and not a few have surfaced in this space. But not very often and not for long.

That's because sooner or later they run up against the same question: what to write about this time? That's when you find out whether or not you're cut out for the work. If you can fill the space, you are a newspaper writer.

I concede that there is no fair way to choose one writer over another. It just happens: you get a phone call, subtle pressure, and the next thing you know, you're in the Sunday newspaper. Reluctant at the start, I now consider it a privilege to be given this forum and have not missed a Sunday, save for medical emergencies, for years.

But how can one manage without a topic? I asked a friend who wrote a popular weekly column, one which was syndicated in a number of newspapers across the country. Each was closely reasoned, lucid, of the right length, and on time. How did he do it? I asked.

"It's simple," he answered. "I shut myself in my office every Wednesday afternoon and don't come out until it's finished. After about two to four hours of swearing at the typewriter you'll find your 700 words."

That was all the information I got out of him and all I needed. That's certainly how I got the job done today.

(6 February 1994)

A sickness in the family is always disruptive. Not only does the affected individual suffer from a variety of discomforts, but the normal flow of things stops or proceeds, if at all, in irregular patterns.

The colds ricocheting among family members since Christmas at our house have given me trouble enough, but I was able to cope until last week. That was when my computer fell ill and my schedule disintegrated.

It wasn't a serious illness: probably the digital equivalent of a nasty head cold. During the worst of it I could still handle correspondence and do some of my radio work. I could even polish off a column. But the computer could no longer "communicate."

Come to think of it, that's what happened to me. After weeks of coughing, my vocal cords quit working and the best I could manage was a croak. Bernadette had the same symptom. Then, in its turn, the computer.

What happened was that the floppy disk drive crashed and I was no longer able to transfer information to or from the hard disk in my machine to others at work. In a sense, the computer could no longer "speak."

So, I called in a computer doctor (they still make house calls) to diagnose and tend my sick machine. Whereas the family practitioner treated me with a variety of pills, the digital doc prescribed surgery: removal and replacement of the affected part.

The operation was quick, effective, and costly. Like Congress, I thought that the president might have been overstating our problems in paying for health care, but there clearly is a crisis in the high cost of treating computers.

While the machine was out of commission, I reflected on the extent to which I have come to depend on it. A part of every day is spent sitting at this keyboard (Hmmm. The keys need cleaning), trying to keep track of things. Almost every aspect of my life has a file in this computer and I would be in real trouble if it truly were to die.

I didn't mean for this to happen. At bottom, I am still a paper kind of guy, filling file cabinets and assorted horizontal surfaces to overflowing with books, documents, letters, fliers: just about everything that results from ink contacting paper.

I bought a computer because everyone else was buying them and the bright young people I knew assured me that I couldn't manage without one. I also purchased a special desk for it, one designed to accommodate the monitor, keyboard, printer and paper in discrete compartments.

I was charmed to learn that the open cabinet above the desk, the section which houses monitor and keyboard, was called a "hutch." That's what I called the cage for my pet rabbit, so I felt that there might be a basis for a relationship.

But then I read the instructions. Some of the words were familiar, but many of them were acronyms I had heard in conversation, but for which I lacked concepts. When mixed into sentences, they made the

whole text incomprehensible, so I closed the manual and went back to my typewriter.

For a considerable period of time, the computer sat alone in an upstairs room, like a monarch on a throne. I would pop in from time to time to admire it and once or twice I turned it on, but only to hear it hum. I had no intention of ever using it.

What deterred me was the assertion, often repeated in my hearing, that computers are dumb. Fast, but dumb. They know nothing but what you tell them; they do nothing but follow your precise orders.

Somehow I knew that this was not true; that my computer was smarter than I and would prove it the minute our wills clashed. So, I left it alone while I continued to calculate by hand and pound the typewriter. I let people know that I had a computer; I just didn't tell them it was strictly ornamental.

In fact, the machine would still be gathering dust if not for this column. I sat down at my IBM Correcting Selectric II one Wednesday night to knock out one of these streams of consciousness when the thing suddenly went into cardiac arrest.

Had I known what kind of resuscitation techniques to use, I would have tried to revive it, but I am not schooled in these matters and could only swear at it. I had to have a column by early the next morning or they would fill my space with another one of those god-awful Mona Charen pieces.

So, I went upstairs to the computer, turned it on, got out the manual, and somehow got it to function as a typewriter. I quickly learned how easy it is to edit and move paragraphs around and, in fact, how it simplifies the whole process. I was hooked.

I had the typewriter repaired, but now it resides in isolation, put to use only for addressing envelopes (I am told that the computer can do this also, but I don't want the typewriter to feel completely abandoned). Everything else goes into the computer.

So, you can understand my panic when it got sick. I had visions of handing in a heavily marked, barely legible manuscript tomorrow as in the old days. But it got out of the hospital this afternoon and is doing just fine.

I'm having a hard time getting it to settle into the old routine, however. All it wants to write about is its operation.

Mostly About My Brother

Pieces of this chapter showed up in two or three columns. They are combined here with some new material.

The last time I saw my brother, David Anthony, Jr., was in 1933. He was almost sixteen; I was four. I wasn't tall enough to see for myself, so someone picked me up to look into his coffin. He was pale and still. I have no real "memory" of the moment; just a sensory snapshot. I can't recall feeling anything. I just looked.

Another snapshot, probably later that day. My mother was sitting in Granddaddy Wooten's room, just off the parlor where David Junior's body was displayed. The lights were out. She held me tightly in her arms as she rocked back and forth, weeping bitterly.

I comprehended nothing. But since my mother was crying, I started crying, too. My head was resting on her shoulder when I saw an angle of light from the parlor. Dad's bald head, fringed in white hair, appeared in the doorway. Then he was standing or kneeling next to us, murmuring "Now, baby; now, baby" over and over.

15

I was to hear that phrase many times in the years to come as he sought to soothe, placate, or reason with mom. Each time, I thought of that moment in Greenwood, Mississippi.

That was where David Junior died. We lived in Memphis, Tennessee, but all of David and Minnie Wooten's kids rotated through Greenwood, usually in the summer, sometimes in pairs, sometimes alone. Charles Chandler Wooten had a sandwich shop there and he lived in a big house on Oak Street with Aunt Rose and Uncle Jake.

By the time Julia and I were taking the train to Greenwood, Granddaddy Wooten was no longer working. He spent most of the day in his rocker, smoking cigars, and reading westerns. It was a pleasant place to visit: a small southern town where life was slow and undemanding — at least for a kid.

In that summer of 1933, David Junior had complained of an abdominal ache and was taken to the doctor. Aunt Rose's physician was out of town, so he was seen by a lesser sort, one who diagnosed malaria as regularly as doctors do acid reflux today. He gave David Junior quinine and sent him home.

By the time Aunt Rose's regular doctor saw him, it was too late. His appendix had ruptured. Word was sent back to mom and dad in Memphis that their son was ill. Mom took the next train; dad and my older sister Marge followed in the one after. Mom got to the hospital in time to see David Junior receive the last rites of the Catholic Church and to die.

I have only three more visual traces of my older brother. Once, when Julia and I were playing outside the family's first-floor apartment, cater-cornered from Central High School, the woman watching us told us to turn around and briefly held us facing the house. When she asked us to turn back, there stood David Junior, tall as a tree, smiling at us.

Another incident is more fragmentary; parts of it have been reconstructed for me by my mother. I was aware of the family getting out a car in front of the Greenwood house. Apparently, I was attracted by the moon and reached out to it. My brother took me and lifted me up as far as he could. I can still see the moon between my outstretched hands. When I discovered that I couldn't grab it, I cried. That brought a round of affectionate laughter which I can still recall.

* * *

Memory is a tricky process. Those who study it tell us that it is a kind of narration. The mind places a familiar picture or action into context for us. What we "see" from the past is a kind of movie with ourselves as one of the actors.

It's as if a touch of schizophrenia were involved. People with such fragmented psyches seem able to see themselves as they interact with others; rather as if parts of their mind were scattered about the room, with one acting as observer.

That's the right brain running things. It's the great story-teller. It creates imaginary playmates for toddlers, lets them hear their voices. After all the neural connections are made between the two halves of the brain, the left brain is firmly in charge at about seven, "the age of reason." The story telling goes on, but in a more subdued fashion, principally in memory.

I discovered just how tricky memory is a few years ago. The family was gathered around the dining-room table and I was reliving a funny incident from years earlier. I recalled taking Teri to get her driver's license. When she got into the car for the driving test, she accidentally backed into a police car, ending the exam for that day. I had a vivid recollection of her muttering under her breath in exasperation rather like a squirrel cussing.

When we had all had a good laugh at her expense, Teri, less amused than the rest, politely informed me that I had been nowhere near the scene. Her older sister, Chris, had taken her to the Secretary of State's office and was the sole family witness.

That was puzzling. Why did I have such a clear memory of the incident? Obviously, Teri was the reliable witness and she was backed up by Chris. How and why did I inject myself into the episode? I guess my right brain thought it was too good a story for me to miss.

That's when I began wondering about those "snapshots" from my earliest years. Were they reconstructions from stories I had heard from my parents and siblings? I started testing them. They were all validated when I was asked, "How did you remember that? You were just a baby!"

Some of them were surprises. When I told my mother of an incident from when I was being weaned, she insisted that it had never happened, But it did. I was there. I saw it.

And that was the final test. Those distant memories did not include me as an actor. What I saw, I saw through my own eyes. Nothing was included beyond my scope of vision. Many things I have never repeated to another living person. Some of them were painful or shameful and I wish I did not recall them. But I do.

* * *

(30 April 2006)

Three a.m. Sleepless in a hospital bed.

I've been here before, listening to familiar night-shift sounds: snores, coughs, a distant cry, subdued laughter from the nurses' station, my own breathing. I remember the first time I heard them, over seventy years ago. I lay in a Memphis, Tennessee, hospital bed, wondering what it was like to die.

The day before, my mom had taken me to see Dr. Carter about my abdominal pains. His initial diagnosis was appendicitis. At the word, mother slumped against the wall and fell to the floor. She had lost her first son, 15-year-old David Junior, to a ruptured appendix about two years earlier.

And so I lay there, awaiting an early morning operation. Mom sat beside me all night, her head in her hands. I knew that appendicitis had taken my brother and wondered if it were going to take me, too.

At first light, the nurse swept into the room, pulled back the covers and told me to get dressed and go home. It turned out that my stomach problems probably stemmed from eating too many apples, a fruit I have largely avoided since.

My early passion for apples developed after an automobile accident in Greenwood: the final "snapshot" I carry of my brother. I was three years old and riding in the rumble seat of a car with another youngster, later identified for me as Bobby Boyce. David Junior was driving, with

Marge in the passenger seat. Bobby climbed out of the rumble seat and hung onto the back of the car. The wind was bothering me, so I slid down to avoid the draft.

A stroke of luck.

The next thing I knew, I was crying in total darkness. David had swerved to avoid a car and driven into a ditch. The rumble seat snapped shut. (I don't know how many people were decapitated by those things before they were taken off the market.) Again, it was an angle of light that caught my attention. I saw David Junior, his face almost as white as when in his coffin, looking down at me in fear. A fold of skin above the corner of my left eye had been pinned by the seat's lid and (as I was told later) was bleeding profusely.

The last part of that episode was a view of Oak Street as I was being carried home in David Junior's arms. I saw my mother hurrying down the front walk, her mouth wide open, her body turned to face us as she ran, almost hopping in her haste. I thought she looked funny.

That was followed by an incident I have recounted numerous times. That's because it made an indelible impression on me; it is one of the sharpest memories from my early years.

They had put me in a crib in the ballroom-sized dining room and members of the family were seated around me talking. Someone brought me an apple. When I tried to bite into it, the stitches over my eye pulled and I started to cry. (Why do so many of these scenes involve crying?)

At that point, Marge reached into the crib and took the apple into the kitchen. I watched her, regretting the loss of the treat. She returned after a short interval and put a plate down in front of me. The apple had been sliced into eight longitudinal parts with the core neatly notched out of each.

I looked at the transformed apple in wonder. I cannot say what, if anything, I thought (I was far too young for any degree of cerebration) but I was aware that something extraordinary had happened. It was the first of several memorable things my older sister was to do for me and, to this day, the most impressive.

The wonder of that moment has stayed with me all my life: a stunning introduction to fractions. For the next three years, I would eat apples no other way and delighted in slicing them myself. As in everything, I overdid it; hence, the abdominal gas pains.

My mind drifted next to my hospital bed at St. Mary's in Humboldt, Tennessee. My high school biology teacher, Sister Amedia, was assigned to be the new hospital's lab technician and she offered me a summer job as her assistant. It was my first extended trip away from home. It was also the very first time I had a bed and room entirely to myself. Until I entered the seminary, I slept on a roll-away cot in the dining room.

I learned how to do the various procedures: urinalysis, blood tests (I found particular pleasure in using the lab microscope for white cell counts) but I drew the line at taking a blood sample from Sister Amedia's arm. "You'll never be a lab tech if you can't do it," she warned. Another career option shot down.

The hospital itself was a curiosity: a Catholic facility in the rural Bible Belt. The mayor came from one of only eight Catholic families in Humboldt. He had convinced the town council that staffing their new facility with hospital nuns would bring them the highest degree of dedication and skill at the most reasonable cost.

But being a recognizable Catholic in that setting wasn't easy. When the nuns walked downtown, people would cross the street to avoid a meeting, but always looked back at them to catch a glimpse of a cloven hoof.

On one occasion, I had to scrub for surgery to help hold down a young woman fighting off anesthesia. She was terrified at the sight of the nuns hovering over her. Not surprisingly, there were few patients that first summer: only the most desperate cases. Thankfully, all survived.

St. Mary's Hospital was divided into three major wings: maternity, general, and colored. As a guilt-ridden Southerner who despised segregation, I insisted on having my room in the colored ward. One of the patients I tended was a youngster who celebrated his fourth birthday there. He was one of the hospital's "miracle" cases: actually recovering from a burst appendix, thanks to newly-developed sulfa drugs.

I spent a lot of time with that kid, delighting in his cure, but I could not turn aside a bittersweet thought that stays with me today. Had this medicine been available 13 years earlier, I would still have an older brother.

Dog Days

Once you get involved with animals, it's hard to quit. I have tried from time to time and have had some success. But not with dogs. Many years ago, a vet at the Thudichum Research Laboratory in Galesburg, Illinois, offered me a half-breed puppy, the result of a stray getting into a pen with his prized Rhodesian Ridgeback.

I took the dog home, named him Beauregard, and he became such a family fixture that, even before his demise, I brought another half-breed into the fold, Loki, a cross between a Norwegian Elkhound mother and a ramblin' father.

And dog followed dog, as dogs do.

(2 April 1989)

Depressing news this week from the nation's capitol.

On the heels of a disastrous oil spill, unrest in the Soviet bloc, and the Ollie North trial, comes news that the presidential pooch has presented the nation with six presidential puppies.

I don't know how that registers with you, but as the owner of a newly acquired, 5-month-old pup, I can tell you that the Bush clan is in for rocky times.

I know the president is busy, but he's got to start training the new arrivals or it won't be safe to walk anywhere in the White House. I'm not sure what method he will use, but I seem to have wound up with one that finds me pacing the lawn several times a day in the company of a creature with boundless energy and no sense of responsibility.

Fenrir (that's his name. It is logical if not euphonious. Our present dog is named Loki, after the Norwegian god with a talent for mischief. Loki's son was Fenrir, a hound of evil nature. We're not very optimistic about our dogs. Where was I?)

Fenrir doesn't take my training seriously. He seems to think that I let him outside to play. What luck we have had in achieving our objectives seems mostly accidental, but the People Who Understand Dogs assure me that, if I just keep at it, sooner or later he will figure things out.

If I'm having this much trouble with one puppy, how is Bush going to cope with six? For openers, he's going to be spreading a lot of paper in one of those basement offices. Of course, he'll be using the Washington Post, so that will give him some enjoyment, but idle amusements eventually pall through repetition.

And who will have to give up precious White House space to accommodate the new arrivals? Making this kind of tough choice could produce a morale crisis among staff members and lead to vicious infighting. Of course, the president could delegate his responsibility in the matter, but that would work against his image as a hands-on kind of guy.

We might accept Reagan sleeping through such a crisis, but we have been led to expect more from Bush.

And, while I don't want to second-guess the image-makers, I might point out that, although pictures of the president nuzzling a puppy might work in the "kinder, gentler" program, it's going to revive some ugly, wimpish memories from the guys down at the union hall.

Caring for the pups could also establish a new fashion trend. After all, everyone watches the president and the slightest change in his attire will have repercussions in the garment district. I know that my appearance has altered. My trousers now sport a fine layer of fur from the knees down and Bush should expect no less.

There is a positive side to all this, however. Some political advantage could accrue. After he has worked with the new litter for a while, Bush may develop some insights useful in dealing with the new Republican House whip, Newt Gingrich of Georgia.

Newt has several puppy-like qualities. He is headstrong, reckless of consequences, given to loud barking for little apparent reason, and likely to make a mess anytime, anywhere. Give him a bone to chew on and he will be content for a while, but he is soon up and nosing about for things to get into.

So, it may be that the president's decision to acquire puppies was not all bad. My experience bears that out. About the time I decide that Fenrir should be traded in for a lawn flamingo, he plants himself on my foot, looks up, and asserts in every motion of his body that I'm an OK guy. No person should be without such support.

No wonder the president has six.

A footnote here for those who insist on logical chronology. While Loki was aging, we acquired Fenrir, a full breed Norwegian Elkhound. Unfortunately, its parents were too closely related and the dog exhibited severe hip displasia. I had to return the pup to the pet store. It was a wrenching experience.

But life goes on.

(10 December 1989)

Today's a big day at our house: this is the day our dog gets a brain. I'm not sure how it happens, but the pet owner's manual we purchased along with the pup stated categorically that we would be wasting our time trying to teach it anything until it was seven months old. The obvious implication was that there would be nothing in her skull to work on until then.

Oh, there must have been at least one brain cell in operation from the beginning, because she has been able to walk, wet, eat, wet, bark, wet, and chew into shreds anything within reach; in addition to wetting.

But today Sigyn is exactly seven months old, so I am assuming that, according to the immutable laws of canine neurological development, sometime last night a second neuron formed in her head and that, as of this moment, she is capable of learning.

This comes in the nick of time, as today is also the day we are installing our Christmas tree and it is essential that she be able to distinguish between the utility of outdoor trees and indoor trees.

I don't want you to think that I have not been trying to teach the pup prior to this moment. Far from it. Ever since I brought her home she and I have been running outside at odd intervals, day and night, to sniff the grass. At least, that seems to be her assessment of the activity.

My confident expectation is that, when we dash out into the chilly dawn this morning, something will click; there will be a flicker across her two-neuron synapse, and a primitive notion will blossom in her brain that all this scurrying about has something to do with sanitation.

I have never been one to push any creature beyond its innate mental endowment, but I hope she learns quickly. It happens that we are unequally prepared for *al fresco* education at this time of year. She is a Norwegian Elkhound, able to survive in arctic snows, while I am a transplanted Southerner, partial to warmth and ease.

Nor am I making unreasonable demands. The only concept I am attempting to convey to her is that certain behaviors are acceptable only in certain environments: that what makes one a "good dog" outside makes one a "BAD DOG!" inside.

The balance of her education is up to our other dog, Loki, who draws on ten years experience as resident pooch to qualify him as a mentor. He is already instructing her in all-night barking, kitchen pan-handling, and year-round shedding: skills he has perfected when not sleeping in front of the fireplace.

We also feel confident that Loki will pass on his considerable ability as a leash-puller. (We do not speak of "taking the dog for a walk" at our house, but of "having the dog take me for a drag.") It requires considerable strength and singleness of purpose to pull a full-grown human uphill at a 45-degree angle, but Sigyn demonstrates the early strength and disposition to follow Loki's example.

What we await almost as anxiously as success in toilet-training is an abatement of nervous energy. There is nothing so relentlessly active as a puppy and what they are bent on is destruction by ingestion. It is hard to imagine an article which has not been pulled from her mouth over the past three months; everything in sight has tiny teethmarks. I am not sure how she managed, but she even devoured my reading glasses.

Loki was like that, too, until he was run over by a van. That slowed him down for a week or two and, afterwards, he appeared to drop vehicles from his list of things to be run down and eaten. We hope that something less traumatic will serve Sigyn as well.

My resolve in this matter is fed by those rare times we enjoy even now, when, for a moment or two, both dogs are content to slump to the floor with me and doze together as we stare into the fire. It will be even better when we can spend those golden intervals admiring the glitter and glow of a fully decorated Christmas tree.

Unless, of course, Sigyn eats it.

(23 May 1993)

Last night I sat down to have another talk with Sigyn. She and I meet for these little heart-to-hearts about once a week to settle arguments and to achieve, through reasoned give-and-take, a harmonious working relationship.

I settle in a comfortable chair while she parks on the rug with her chin on my knee, her liquid, brown eyes staring at me intently, framing the unspoken question "Are we out of popcorn?"

Sigyn is the third dog we have had in the family. Actually, the fourth, if you count King, a runaway German shepherd lured into the house by our children many years ago.

At the time, we considered the children a sufficient source of annoyance, so we shopped around for King's owner or a foster-owner. The dog was taken off our hands by a Rock Island policeman after it had lived with us for only two or three weeks.

He was not quickly forgotten, however. One can still read messages chalked on attic beams by the older children who were just learning to write and who used this rudimentary skill to record their undying devotion to King as well as the depth of their feelings about stony-hearted parents.

I have never erased or painted over these sentiments. I have even cleared a little space in front of them so I can stand and read them. I plan to carry a small desk up there one of these days so that I can keep them in view as I write my will.

But back to Sigyn. What I have been trying to get across to her is that a distinction should be made between dogs and people. It matters little to us if a dog walks by our home, but Sigyn seems to think it an occasion of significant concern.

She acknowledges the presence of any creature within 75 feet of the house by barking vigorously and charging to the nearest window. But her reaction quickly accelerates into full-blown panic if the intruder is another dog.

In this high emotional state she will lunge at doors and windows and, if we have left the front door open, try to burst through the screen door. In this manic condition, she somehow confuses the people who visit us regularly — postman, newspaper carrier, our sons — with other dogs.

As you can imagine, this provokes an equally earnest response on my part, so that energy levels can become quite high on these occasions.

So it is that I try to reason with her from time to time, stressing the fact that we have little interest in passing animals, and reminding her that it is highly unlikely that she will ever receive a letter if she continues to treat the postal carrier in such hostile manner.

She is an earnest participant in these discussions, but I fear her mind is on popcorn most of the time. When it becomes apparent that no food is forthcoming, she will simply push her head under my hand in a mute request to have her ears scratched.

This failure to communicate stems, no doubt, from the fact that I had little to do with Sigyn's early training. Oh, I got up every morning to take her outside, but it took three months for her to figure out why. Impatient with this slow progress, I left the balance of her education to Loki.

Loki was dog number two (or three, if you read the attic runes) and he had learned his responsibilities from his predecessor, Beauregard. Loki was an exceptionally bright animal who seemed to have such a positive fix on his role in the home that I seldom interfered with his decisions.

Loki passed on to Sigyn his aggressive stance as a watchdog, but died before Sigyn had learned to make critical distinctions between friend and foe, or had learned that "Quiet!" was a sound which conveyed a specific meaning.

I have been told that my conversational approach to the problem is all wrong; that dogs need discipline, routine, and consistency. I know the words, but have trouble with the concepts. I think it all goes back to a brief scene in my childhood when I chanced upon an old man in a battered automobile who was traveling around with six or eight mongrel dogs. He had stopped in a parking lot near the hotel my dad managed and I went over to see what he was doing.

He had a command of those scruffy dogs that was little short of miraculous. They would walk on their hind legs, play hide-and-seek, balance balls or sticks on their noses, count, do flips; almost anything that the old man asked them to do.

I was amazed by this and tried to figure out how a person could establish that kind of rapport with an animal. I hung around after his impromptu performance and watched. He talked to the dogs and they seemed to answer him. They obviously slept in the same car and probably shared the same fleas. They had a closeness that amounted to kinship.

I finally deduced that the dogs obeyed him because they loved him and he loved them. I learned in later years that this isn't quite how it works, but I was fatally warped by that first judgment.

So I conclude by assuring Sigyn of my affection, emphasize my hopes for her improved behavior, suggest that we both try to think before we act, then go to the kitchen to pop some corn.

(2 November 1997)

"Vanum est vobis ante lucem surgere."

That Latin phrase from 50 years ago has been running through my mind lately. I don't know its source; I have sometimes imagined it to be a friendly admonition from Cicero, or one of Tertullian's precepts for the early Christian Church.

But setting it down on paper, I sense a less exalted origin: probably a fellow seminary student with a rudimentary knowledge of Latin. One who was as dismayed as I to hear Basil Perrino ringing that blasted bell every morning at 5 a.m., summoning us to a very sleepy morning meditation.

The English version depends on how sharply you wish to translate *vanum*. It is usually transliterated as "vanity," but you may also use stronger terms, such as empty or foolish.

But when you are roused from a warm bed on a cold morning in total darkness, I think you can state it only one way: "It's really stupid to get up before sunrise."

That's what I have been doing for the past two weeks: getting up ahead of the sun. For a night person, one who is accustomed to retiring around 2 a.m., this is a serious matter.

And what draws me from my repose at such an ungodly hour? A belated attempt to live my life according to the rule of St. Benedict? Nothing of such noble intent, I fear.

I am attempting to housebreak yet another three-month-old puppy.

The latest addition to our household is, you guessed it, a Norwegian Elkhound, one we purchased from Jon and Harriette Bell who live near Tipton, Iowa. This, in spite of my repeated protestations that I would never own a dog of that breed again.

Understand, the Elkhound is a noble beast, an excellent watchdog with uncommonly keen hearing and a ferocious bark. However, it is not perfect in all respects. It has a very thick coat which it sheds twice a year. As the one who wields the vacuum cleaner at our house, I find this a matter of considerable annoyance. On some Saturdays, it seems that I am gathering up enough hair to constitute another dog.

So, I had sworn that the next dog would be one more closely attached to its coat. I had started thumbing through some canine publications and had begun thinking seriously about a Labrador. But fate took a hand; a rather cruel hand. Sigyn, the resident pooch for the last eight years, developed an inoperable cancer and, for the first time in 30 years, we were suddenly without a dog.

Riding the emotional tide of Sigyn's demise, we checked the ads for a puppy and saw that nine Norwegian Elkhound pups were available. Resolutions went out the window as Bernadette and I drove over to examine the litter.

Truth to tell, we wanted them all. But knowing what lay ahead, we selected just one; Freia (Well, what kind of names do you expect? They're Norwegian after all) and promised to pick her up a month later.

What prompted us to let her stay on the farm was the imminent arrival of our grandchildren. As much as kids and dogs go together, I was not willing to throw them together when potty-training was still an active issue on both sides.

So, the day after the grandchildren left, we rode out to Tipton, picked up Freia, and returned home as quickly as possible (turns out the pup was prone to car-sickness). Since then I have been leaping out of bed at the first soft whimper from downstairs. Out she goes and — *mirabile dictu!* (I do know some legitimate Latin phrases) — comprehends what these outdoor trips are for.

In that respect, it's been rather an easier adjustment than with pups of the past. However, both of us had forgotten at what high energy levels a young dog operates. Or how thoroughly it investigates every corner of the house it can reach. Or how sharp small teeth and claws are and how readily and forcefully they are used. Many things are taking on that slightly tattered look which betrays the presence of a dog, including us.

But matters are settling down nicely. I have gotten Freia an old sweatshirt and outworn tennis shoes to chew on. She accepts the enclosed porch as her bedroom. She gives us an appropriate warning when she wishes to go out. And she is already a great watchdog.

Her hearing is acute and her bark is strong. She is a fine replacement for Sigyn and Loki, Elkhounds which preceded her. We haven't forgotten those splendid companions, of course, because we still see them in Freia's darkened muzzle and eyes.

Admittedly, the timing could be better — training will proceed into the depths of winter, I fear, and I will still be getting up early for the next three months.

But, *vanum* or not, it's something I am committed to doing; rising early once again to pray, not for personal spirituality, but for a well-behaved dog.

Katrina Comes Calling

During most of my two dozen years in television, I stood in front of a U.S. map twice a day and speculated about the weather. While not a meteorologist, I played one on TV. In the process, I made a number of friends at the local weather bureau and learned a lot about how it all works.

I guess that's why I stay tuned to the weather channel when no football game is available. As you can imagine, I was riveted by the devastating storms which savaged the Gulf Coast in 2005.

(4 September 2005)

Along with the rest of the country, I have logged many hours in front of the television set, watching the surprising development and subsequent, devastating impact, of Hurricane Katrina.

From a disorganized low south of Bermuda, it grew into an easily predictable, minimal hurricane destined to cross South Florida and then slide up that state's west coast.

But an unanticipated swing out into the Gulf of Mexico gave it a chance to make history and it did; feeding off the hot gulf water until it was ready to outdo Camille in Gulf Coast destruction and fulfill the dire predictions often made for New Orleans.

I remember the first time I visited the Big Easy. After strolling to St. Louis Cathedral and wolfing beignets at Cafe du Monde, I walked up a long flight of steps to the top of the Mississippi River levee. The view was disorienting.

The long walk up was balanced by a short walk down to the river's edge. Looking from one side of the levee to the other, it was obvious that the city was in continual peril of flooding. It was many feet below sea level.

Both there and later at Lake Ponchartrain I had the sense that, sooner or later, that brawling, bawdy bowl of a town would be filled with water. This year, it was.

Television reporters have a natural (and unbecoming) tendency to exaggerate events. They want, not so much to inform, as to raise hackles, induce tears, get some kind of emotional response for their viewers. It's good for ratings.

But sometimes nature does their work for them and that was the case along the central Gulf Coast this week. The scale of the disaster is beyond a quick sound bite or the collective observations of reporters, strung out along the coast like sentinels.

It is still impossible to get it all into one comprehensible frame. The telephones don't work, not even cell phones. Computers are useless: no electricity, no net linkages. Roads are blocked, bridges are down. Authorities at all levels can't get a handle on things: there is no reliable means of collecting information.

The public response has been immediate, but not immediately effective. People stranded in the hot sun need water at once; food very soon. The sick and incapacitated need more than the one functioning hospital to tend to their needs.

Once again, as in the Asian tsunami, nature has demonstrated how quickly it can throw even the most highly developed society into confusion. Our instruments of convenience — cars, communication devices — quickly become irrelevant when nature breaks out in fury.

A note in Nature magazine last week commented that scientists who study the weather are beginning to identify an unsettling tendency in storms of all kinds. It seems that when the elements combine to produce what we call weather, they take the most violent course open to them. Some people are like that.

No matter how engrossing the subject under treatment, television coverage leaves you with plenty of idle time for the mind to wander. For example, I noticed that bad weather usually produces an increase in commercials on the weather channel and news specials.

Madison Avenue's reasoning is simple: more people watch when danger looms, so let's get their attention for our product as well. But the contrast between the real suffering of human beings in the news and the irrational perkiness of people from the Television Planet would seem to undercut an ad's effectiveness. Perhaps I watch too closely, too critically.

But then, I want to know what happened to my friends who live along the coast, from whom we have heard nothing. With my focus on them, I not only have no interest in Labor Day Sales; I don't want to hear about them.

I also think how badly we have bungled the oil situation, what with the senseless attack on Iraq and the subsequent unreliability of that supply; our attempts to bring down Hugo Chavez' government in Venezuela; our unwillingness to promote conservation at home: all have made the disruption of our national sources that much more critical.

This, in turn, draws one's attention to the Great Problem in Capitalism. If gasoline is temporarily in short supply, jack up the price and make as much money as you can. It's okay; we call it Supply and Demand. It's happening all across the country, even where the supply is under no immediate threat; public perception offers an excuse.

Meanwhile, out in the Atlantic, another storm is brewing.

(11 September 2005)

There must be other things going on in the world, but they have been shunted from the headlines by Hurricane Katrina and the collapse of a city, a region, and the myth of American competence.

It's a natural for television: displaced families, lost relatives, bodies floating in polluted waters, poor people unwilling to leave their water-logged homes, dramatic aerial shots of flooded streets and vanished neighborhoods.

But it's not just television. National Public Radio has done some stunning reporting from the field; newspapers around the world have dispatched teams to the region; even cable news outlets have managed to shed their political bias and react with outrage to the reality on the ground.

Horror stories are filtering out of the gulf coast. Some of them are rumors (rapes, armed mobs, murdered children), but each day brings a documented atrocity, from the physical (a nursing home filled with corpses) to the political (FEMA's slo-mo orders for its staff to visit New Orleans to provide an appearance of activity).

As I say, it has been a dominating story and deservedly so. We haven't seen anything like this since the great Mississippi River Flood of 1927. No, I wasn't alive then, but I heard about it growing up and witnessed its effects on the land (mass migrations north) and in government (The New Deal).

The streets are not yet dry in the Big Easy, but the blame game is already in full swing. Everyone from President Bush to New Orleans' Mayor Nagin is taking heat. Some commentators imaginatively chose to blame the welfare state. Rush Limbaugh, typically, blames President Clinton. But most of the fire is aimed at the Department of Homeland Security and the Federal Emergency Management Agency.

The collapse of FEMA has been spectacular. It was one of the brightest achievements of the Clinton years. James Lee Witt transformed that agency into a model of efficiency and competence, earning bi-partisan praise. Now, it has been lost in the Homeland Security shuffle and many of its professionals are gone, replaced by political time-servers.

In addition to the finger-pointing, many thoughtful people are looking beyond the Gulf disaster and the shabby response to it to address deeper issues. Once again, we have laid bare the gulf between black and white, rich and poor, north and south, the comfortable and the exposed.

There are many important issues in play just now, but they are lost in the aftermath of Katrina. Some think the storm may reverse the tide against big government. Others think a sophisticated public relations campaign from the White House will wash it from our collective memory.

Still others believe it has left George Bush singularly exposed as a man who simply occupies the office, while letting Dick Cheney, Donald Rumsfeld and others do the heavy lifting. (They cite the fact that the entire Bush team was also on vacation during the hurricane, leaving the president stuck in his schedule without someone to give him directions.)

While I hold no brief for the president, I don't think he is stupid. But I am convinced that he lacks curiosity, imagination, and a passion for public service. Like many privileged children, he has had too much done for him all his life. He is disconnected from the experience of ordinary Americans.

But, in this instance, I think he is primarily the victim of White House procedures. Nothing there is done quickly; everything is planned, meticulously arranged to set him in friendly environments. It takes time to get it right, to assure that he looks and sounds confident and presidential. Unfortunately, the Gulf disaster is something more consequential than a photo op.

(18 September 2005)

While we are still dealing with hurricanes, past and present — Katrina, Ophelia, and whatever is currently brewing out in the Atlantic — many are already starting to talk seriously about the future of the city hardest hit this year: New Orleans; specifically, if it is to be rebuilt.

It seems unthinkable that such a special urban center might be allowed to dwindle into insignificance. Not only is it a vital port for international trade, it is also a place of unusual historic and cultural importance.

House Speaker Dennis Hastert spoke bluntly about the unacceptable cost of trying to restore the Big Easy. (It's unacceptable to him because it is not in his district.) Still, he has a point. It could prove to be the costliest salvage job in our history.

But it's not only the opposition of Speaker Hastert and others which presents a deterrent to getting New Orleans up and running again; Mother Nature seems to be against restoration as well.

First of all, the below-sea-level city is a physical affront to both ocean and river. Without human intervention, much of the place would be permanently under water. Next, there are those recurring hurricanes, which test human ingenuity from time to time, reminding us that wind, wave, and gravity are not to be taken lightly.

But the real force working against New Orleans is the Mississippi River. It's not that it wants to shut the place down; it just wants to be somewhere else.

If you've spent any time on the lower Mississippi, you know how it has looped around over the years, cutting off channels and scouring out new ones. As a boy scout in Memphis, I got to make a number of boat trips through "old water," nosing through shallow, overgrown places to enter into broad stretches that used to be part of the main channel.

For a long time now, the Mississippi has wanted to leave its Baton Rouge-New Orleans route and cut through the Atchafalaya River, emptying into the Gulf through western Louisiana. Oddly enough, it was helped along by the Corps of Engineers.

Centuries ago, the Red River was a tributary of the Mississippi, but was plugged up by a 100-mile-long log jam. The Atchafalaya had also been clogged through some thirty miles of its main channel by a prehistoric log jam.

Captain Henry Shreve, superintendent of the Corps of Engineers, undertook to clear up and make navigable both the Red and Atchafalaya. This allowed the Atchalafaya to capture the Red River as its own tributary.

Through "old river" channels, it also had links with the Mississippi and the Father of Waters started to donate some of its abundance to the revived river. As floods came and went, more and more water began to end up in the Atchafalaya.

This was recognized as a threat to the heavily-industrialized Baton Rouge-New Orleans corridor. A ton of money has been invested in that area. A change in the Mississippi's main channel would deal a devastating blow to regional economy.

So, the corps built the Old River Floodway, 50 miles north of Baton Rouge, to regulate the flow of Mississippi water westward. It has worked so far, but was nearly undercut by a major flood a few years ago. With another really big one, the Mississippi may well bypass that barrier and establish a new main channel into the Gulf of Mexico.

This fascinating bit of river history is worth examining. If you can find a detailed map of Louisiana, you will see for yourself the tangle of channels and easily trace where the Mississippi River would like to go, if left to its own devices.

Of course, it has had help. Everyone understands how the system of locks, dams, and levees has turned the Mississippi into a torrent which constantly threatens to escape its confines.

The original plan for managing the river included, not only levees, but overflow areas which would let water stretch out when under pressure. Unfortunately, that part of the plan was never well implemented.

I'm sure there was no malicious intent in the project which cleared the Atchafalaya and Red Rivers and cut channels through old river meanders. The Corps of Engineers just didn't realize how tempting the new outlet might be for the Mississippi.

We are always trying to improve on Nature and always with the best of intentions. But we have a bad habit of pursuing short-term goals, often with only a hazy notion of what might happen further down the line.

As we have learned anew this year, water will go where it wants.

(25 September 2005)

Watching the weather channel this Wednesday, I marvel at the growing immensity of Hurricane Rita. Outer bands are flicking the Gulf Coast from Florida to Louisiana, which has to make Katrina survivors nervous.

I finally got an e-mail from a friend who weathered Katrina in a small town just east of Biloxi. She and her daughter were lucky; their apartment was one foot above the storm surge. They would have been better off staying there.

As it was, they went to a three-story church building, trusting in God and the higher structure. When the water came up to the second floor, they went higher and started looking for ropes, cords, anything to lash themselves to something solid.

Out the window, she saw people she knew crawl from their upper-story window into a tree, where they stayed while their home crumbled and floated away. Seventy percent of the town was leveled: "The devastation is so much greater than the television coverage can possibly convey."

She is lucky, now in a dry apartment, "blessed with water, ice, power (finally), food (a pantry full of canned goods and MREs). I can't say enough for the American Red Cross and don't even want to mention FEMA." Her frustration with FEMA verges on the volcanic.

Best of all, she was called back to work and paid for the week she was sweating out the hurricane. The news there was bleak: "Thirteen of the people I work with had lost everything, many more were flooded out, and one death has occurred due to ingesting toxic bacteria from the tidal surge."

Watching and reading about the disaster reminded me of a comment by one of my children many years ago when we were safe inside as a ferocious winter storm raged outside: "I'm so glad we have a home."

I also think of the time my two younger daughters fled from their trailer home in Florida as a roaring fire quickly consumed everything they had; everything but the clothes they were wearing. I wonder how I would cope with such an overwhelming loss.

My home is stuffed with the things I have accumulated over 55 years in this town: files and cartons crammed with papers — some, important — boxes of photographs, art works (enough by Bill Hannan alone to fill a gallery), recordings, books in sufficient number to support the house if the walls fail, furniture, clothes — the list is beyond my reckoning. (It's a very big house).

Now, another storm gathers strength in the middle of the Gulf Coast and dithers about where to spend its incalculable energy. (A wicked thought: What if it headed straight for Crawford, Texas? How would the politically pious interpret that, after identifying Katrina as God's judgment on sinful old New Orleans?)

This same night, a tornado ventures into neighborhoods just north of Minneapolis. Nature seems to be kicking up a fuss as we cross from summer into autumn and one is tempted to read something into it all.

I know better, of course. As the earth warms, weather reacts in a more violent manner. The science is clear, although we still have a ways to go to wrap our heads around all the details.

Weather will do what it will do. We have contributed to the mix of elements which form it, with acid rain, fossil fuel emissions, soil erosion, land "reclamation," and the cavalier attitude that the earth belongs, not to all life, but just to us and we can do with it whatever we damned well please.

What good fortune brought me to this settled place? I live beyond the hurricane's full fury, on the extreme outer reaches of the New Madrid Fault, well above the Mississippi's surge (I think); subject only to the hazard of a tornado, from which terror modern forecasting techniques offer me, if not safety, then at least a chance to duck and cover.

I have lolled by the ocean's edge, admired the shallow serenity of the Gulf Coast, and day-dreamed about the salubrious island breezes of the South Pacific, but I have no desire to live in these places. I am rooted in the Midwest and want to stay here.

Perhaps the Quad-Cities is not your idea of Eden — come to think of it, it isn't mine, either — but it's a great place to live. I fell in love with this juncture of the Rock and Mississippi Rivers the first time I saw it and never imagined leaving. It is my home.

It is also the community which has given me my wife, family, and friends; opportunities to work, to teach, to serve. The attachments are many; one of the strongest of which is simply the place itself.

If you don't share the feeling immediately, think about it for a while. This is a satisfying place in which to live. As my Gulf Coast friend concluded in her e-mail: "My plan is to move back to Illinois next May. Enough!!!"

The March of Time

Time passes, often without drawing attention to itself. But occasionally, a glance in a mirror will bring me up short: What is my father doing in there?

(27 March 1994)

On March 15th, I finally took my birth certificate down to the Social Security Office and admitted that I was going to turn sixty-five the next day.

I had already bought a cane, a shawl, and inquired into the availability of wheelchairs. I put in a stock of oatmeal as a prelude to gruel and have taken up a regimen of vitamins. Thus armed, I stepped into official old age.

Bernadette sent me to the SS office. She knew the ropes, having had invaluable experience dealing with the elderly. She had been a specialist in the field down at Information and Referral before United Way decided their staff needed jobs more than the community needed the service.

She told me to sign up for Medicare "A" (whatever that is) and to refuse Medicare "B" for the present as I am still employed and have insurance coverage. Otherwise, I was simply to follow instructions.

Lisa Schillig, a pleasant and genuinely lovely young woman, was the staffer assigned to my case. I imagine they had drawn lots and that she had lost. At the touch of a key she called up my past and asked questions which, fortunately for my pride, touched only on money.

The money part did surprise me a bit: it didn't add up to much. I was sure I had taken in a million by now. After all, I started working at age 14 and had been on someone's payroll continuously for 51 years. I now realize that when job satisfaction is what you're looking for, that's likely all you'll get.

Anyway, everything she needed was there, except that the 1982 figure was wrong. I have to look up my tax return for that year and have the record corrected. Then, I will be properly enrolled as a senior citizen, a golden oldie, one of the folks for whom popular music is not written.

It has been an interesting process, this aging business. I haven't paid much attention to it, although I have noticed its side effects from time to time.

My forehead is much higher than it used to be and what hair remains up there is passing from gray to white. My chest seems to have slumped into my waist and my knees, which used to make loud noises when I walked up the stairs, are now silent, but less flexible.

While I still venture out into the world on some nights, most of the time I am content to watch TV after dinner until falling asleep. I am nodding off earlier and earlier; it's been a while since I've watched McNeil/Lehrer all the way through.

I am usually back to work by 8 p.m., but I find I am spending more nights at my desk on the front porch or at the upstairs computer than at the radio station. And I get distracted more easily. I will remember a quote or article and spend hours idling through the accumulated litter of a lifetime in search of it.

By the way, I usually have some notion where such things can be found between attic and basement. On the other hand, I haven't a clue as to the location of my tax returns.

I really must be getting up there. When I was a child, I couldn't imagine living past forty: that seemed incredibly old. Some people I admired had finished their productive work as well as their lives in their thirties (Jesus and Mozart come most readily to mind) so there seemed little point in hanging around after that.

I fact, I didn't really grow up until the age of thirty. It was only then that I began to trust my judgment. And by that time I was married, had five kids, had established the Genesius Guild, and was settled into the communications field. It must have been luck; it certainly was not the election of a mature mind.

But sixty-five can't be ignored. For most of my life, that has been the normal retirement age. In some occupations, it was mandatory. Only in recent times have people consented to the notion that you can work past that limit.

Of course, it never applied to artists. They were the special class exempted from any number of rules, retirement being a big one. Stokowski was conducting in his nineties and legions of painters got better as their eyesight failed.

The real puzzle is that nothing seems to have changed inside. Apart from digestion, I mean. The mind not only does not accept aging, it doesn't even recognize it away from a mirror. I am still impatient to get things done, although I don't let delays anger me as much as they did in the past.

I like to think I have become more understanding. It was the gift I hoped age would bring, but I can't be sure. I still have trouble accepting fools and charlatans. Rush Limbaugh and Pat Robertson cannot count on me to swell their ratings.

Mostly it means little. If it weren't for the cards and kind thoughts from family and friends, my sixty-fifth trip around the sun would merit no attention at all.

Except, of course, from the government, which takes note and rewards my longevity by letting a charming young lady remind me, ever so gently, that I am getting close enough to the end of life to give it some thought.

(19 October 1997)

There are a number of ways to measure a life.

The most common usage is a division of linear time: we are so many years old; so many trips taken around the sun on planet earth. This can be uncomfortably precise. We generally prefer to use vague terms such as young and old.

When you start dividing these generalities, you wind up with a number of subsets. At the early end of the scale, there are infants, toddlers, pre-schoolers, kindergartners, youngsters, pre-teens, teenagers, and adolescents, a term that, in our time, has become sufficiently elastic to include people in their fifties.

Speaking of maturity, grown-ups cannot reach a consensus as to what "middle age" really means. If the average life span is 70, then 35 is

definitely the middle number; but I challenge you to find anyone in his or her thirties who thinks middle age appropriate to them.

As the population ages and the number of post-39 people balloons, "middle age" seems to stretch all the way up to AARP membership.

Living, as we do, in a culture that has a perverse fixation on youth, old age is even trickier to deal with than middle age. To begin with, what do you call folks like myself (within the bounds of decency, of course) who are shouldering up against our allotted three-score-and-ten?

Are we seniors, golden oldies, the elderly, gaffers and crones, venerable ones, or the pre-deceased? Clearly, there are differences within age groupings; distinctions that cannot be drawn simply by counting the candles on a birthday cake.

I am surprised how touchy people get about such things. You have only to watch that universal arbiter of contemporary life, television, to see what I mean.

I refer, in particular, to the snotty TV ads that draw invidious distinctions between old folks who spend their time scuba diving (thanks to ingestion of vitamins or patent medicines or — unbelievably — the counsel of some stock broker) and those who sit peacefully on the beach (my personal idea of a high old time).

It can be difficult to convey the fact of a person's incipient antiquity without giving offense. Everyone must find his or her own way out of this verbal thicket. Almost any euphemism you employ is going to upset the Older Generation and trigger denial, indignation, or both.

The surprising fact is that few of us really age inside. We may have acquired some patience and prudence along the way, but a lot of the interior landscape remains familiar, if not precisely the same.

Personally, I can't find a whole lot of internal difference between the ideas, enthusiasms, and energy of my sixteenth year and my sixtieth. What changes the equation is that body parts are wearing out. I occasionally forget that the knees that carried me through a thousand games of touch football can barely get me out of a chair.

I may not have Joe Namath's memories, but I share his partiality for sitting often and long.

So, what should I call myself now that no one mistakes me for a kid anymore? "Gaffer" and "coot" seem a bit harsh; but what else is there?

Well, let the Bureau of Vital Statistics, the Department of Social Security, or the tolerant children who populate the police force, hospitals, and suchlike call me what they will. I know what I am and am content to be:

Around.

(26 July 1998)

Last Sunday, I was walking along the brow of the hill in Lincoln Park, back of the crowd at the classic theatre, when something caught my eye.

I suppose I should have been watching the play more closely, but I had seen the first performance the night before and, anyway, a director's job is over after dress rehearsal. After that, it's pretty much a matter between actors and audience.

What I had spotted was a branch, obviously from one of those impressive oaks which fill the park. It was about two-and-a-half feet long, about an inch thick, and slightly bent in the middle.

Perhaps it was the shape — one which suggested a boomerang — that gave me the impulse. I had a sudden urge to pick it up and sail it into the ravine which curves down from the hill.

You know the feeling. It is strongest at the edge of a pond or river. You instinctively start digging around for a flat stone to skip over the water.

But I merely looked at the stick, glanced down the ravine, and continued to walk. I hadn't taken two steps when a boy of about five came racing along, spotted the stick, and, without a second's hesitation, sailed it down the hill.

I watched it settle about half-way down. "I could have gotten it a lot farther," I thought. As I moved away, the boy started searching for another stick to follow the first.

Now, why that image has stayed with me this week is hard to explain. Perhaps it has something to do with the distance between youth and old age. It might just as well be a parable about impulse and self-control. Maybe it is nothing more than a distinction to be drawn between abundant energy and chronic fatigue.

Most likely, I am vaguely irritated that the kid wasn't burdened with a second thought. Like Macbeth, he acted immediately upon his impulse: "The very firstlings of my heart shall be the firstlings of my hand."

Of course, kids can get away with stuff like that. No one expects them to be responsible. But am I confusing responsibility with stuffiness? What's wrong with acting like a kid from time to time? With taking a short vacation from maturity?

The truth is, I long ago abandoned spontaneity. I have tried to learn, from a sometimes painful past, to think before I speak or act. The trouble is that I have never worked out the proper balance. My timing is usually off.

I have waited well past the appropriate time as often as I have spoken or acted prematurely. Whatever the perfect moment is, I seem to miss it consistently. Sometimes you can make it up; often, you can't. Rather like the bashful boy who can't get up the nerve to tell a girl he loves her until she is engaged to someone else.

But then, what's the big deal? The kid did something that I merely thought about. Perhaps it's just another reminder that a lot of time has passed; that I am a long way from such carefree days; that I really ought to unbend and enjoy my second childhood.

Wait till I find another stick.

(20 June 1998)

In my life-long quest to live Just One More Day, I have developed some specific rules I consider essential to a long and pleasant existence: chief among them, to eat at least one of the Three Basic Food Groups — Ice Cream, Popcorn, and Hot Dogs — every day.

So it was that, during a steamy noon hour last week, I drove over to Country Style in Moline for a vanilla, soft-serve cone. I then motored a short distance to the fence west of Browning Field to park in the shade and enjoy my medicine.

With nothing to occupy my mind but gustatory delight, I looked over at the field and saw two young men trotting around the track. I judged them to be in their late teens and in good physical condition. They would have to be, to be exercising in the hot sun.

At the far end of the track, they stopped and moved into the infield. There, for as long as I watched, they engaged in a series of quick maneuvers: running forward, scuttling sideways, then quickly backpedaling: moves you associate with defensive backs or linebackers in football.

Sometime they alternated exercises; first one racing forward and back, then the other. Sometimes they moved together; now facing forward; again, watching each other closely. Nothing complicated, but precise and obviously patterned to develop specific skills.

I kept that image in my mind for the rest of the day. What impressed me was the utter seriousness with which they went about their drills. Each routine was done three times and each sequence was timed. They weren't exercising just for the fun of it; they had a goal in mind: making the team or moving to the top of the depth chart.

When you're that age, energy is what you have to spare. And, when you really want something, you'll spend that energy prodigally. But why, I wondered, is it almost always spent on sports?

True, it is a wonderfully exhilarating thing to dwell in the muscles: to race until your breath is spent; to leap into the air to snag a football; stretch to intercept a dribble; or feel the release of tension as the bat connects with the ball.

I used to play punt and pass with Jack Acerra until it got too dark to see the ball. I never walked when I could run. For the first 21 years of my life, I was always ready to play some game and, until I wrenched my shoulder in a volleyball game thirty years ago, could easily be talked into a quick game of touch football.

Ideally, that kind of stuff is its own reward. But we have institutionalized sports to such an extent that it overshadows almost everything else a growing person might do. True, we work to see that academic ability is honored as well, but public enthusiasm for athletics doesn't need promoting; it dominates.

And it's the domination that bothers me. We have made such a fetish of sports excellence that it can get a youngster's life out of balance. Think how many kids, admiring Michael Jordan, spend hours practicing lay-ups and three-pointers, honing a skill that will ultimately prove meaningless.

There is only one Michael Jordan. There are only a few hundred who can stay in the game with him. For the rest, it's time largely wasted. Oh, it may keep your body in tone, develop spatial judgment, and increase lung capacity, but shooting baskets during most of your free time doesn't mean much in the adult world.

The best thing that can happen to a youngster is to grow in an environment in which all human faculties are equally valued. Where games are simply games, where learning is more in the mind than in the muscles, where social skills extend beyond team sports, where self-discipline is acquired from the arts as well as from organized play.

I don't know where to find such an educational Utopia, but I suspect that Horace Mann School in Rock Island comes close. That's the school where kids study year-round and what brings it to mind is that the first group of kids who have attended since grade one have just graduated.

What I don't understand is why there isn't a massive public outcry for all local schools to adopt the Horace Mann model. In a future in which mental training will mean far more than athletic competition, a year-round curriculum would seem essential.

The long summer break is a unique anachronism of American education, established when schooling was considered less important than summer work in the fields. The world's priorities have changed, but the school schedule remains mired in the past.

Kids are impressionable. They adopt their values, not only from what they see and hear, but from what they experience. Going to school all year long, with several short breaks, keeps the life of the mind in focus. The fantasy world of rich, reckless athletes will always be in the news, but the day-by-day experience of study in a supportive setting will ground them in a more satisfying reality.

I hope those two young men who ventured into the heat of mid-day to hone their athletic skills spend an equal amount of time developing their critical faculties, broadening their knowledge of this marvelous world, and speculating on the riddle of life.

They're going to need something to sustain them when muscle turns to lard, when others have taken their place on the team, when their noontime preoccupation simplifies to an ice cream cone.

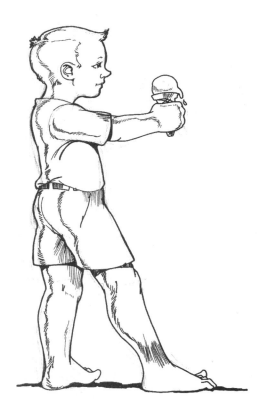

Class Reunion

For reasons I cannot identify, I never attended a class reunion of any kind. Then I got this telephone call ...

(1 August 1993)

Father Time rang me up this Wednesday. He said his name was John Coletta and he was calling to invite me to attend a reunion of St. Thomas grade school graduates from 1943.

Since I have never been quick with numbers, it took me a few moments to realize that he was asking me to admit, by showing up at a dinner on Aug. 28, that it has been fully 50 years since I got my grade school diploma.

Not only did the invitation remind me just how much of my life has been used up, it also got me to thinking about the 50 to 60 kids with whom I spent my formative years. While my memory has declined along with other faculties, I have a better image of that group than of my high school or college classmates.

Most of them were Italian and names like Lucchesi, Leone, Pretti, Belenchi, Pirani, Benedetti, and Acerra sounded as natural to me as Smith and Jones. We also had a sprinkling of Irish, some of whom were Irish Travelers who lived in a tent encampment on the edge of town.

My relationship with those kids was a bit unusual. From the fourth grade on, I was often asked to monitor the class or even assist in teaching while the sister was busy doing something else. It seemed perfectly natural at the time; odd only in retrospect.

Another curious fact of my life at St. Thomas was that I rarely went out to play at recess or lunchtime, especially during the first three grades. I was told that I had to stay in because I was susceptible to colds. I found out later that I had developed a heart murmur and that Mom was worried that strenuous play might deprive her of a second son (my older brother died at age 15).

When I did venture forth, the schoolyard seemed a wholly different society, with rules made up by kids. My three-year absence from daily play left me woefully deficient in the subtleties of various games; one which took years to make up. It didn't damper my enthusiasm; merely my competence.

I cannot claim total recall of those times, only isolated instances, such as the time we staged a wartime playlet in which I portrayed Hitler in my Boy Scout uniform with a lank triangle of hair over my right eye. Jimmy Pirani depicted Mussolini. I forget who Hirohito was; possibly Isadore Johnson.

Isadore lived up the street from me. After leaving grade school, he was sent to a military school in eastern Tennessee. We linked up again at St. Ambrose seminary, where I discovered his first name had been legally changed to Warren. That struck me as an amazingly bold assertion of independence at a tender age and I admired his daring.

From grades one through six, I was deeply in love with June Williams. She lived in a fine brick house on Parkway and seemed, somehow, to have come from a different world. I can't explain it, but her coloring, appearance, and manner seemed to bespeak an aristocratic background and made her the unattainable princess of my dreams.

Maggie Acerra was closer. She lived right next door (we rented from her mother) and, in the back of my mind, I assumed that we would marry one day if I didn't go to the seminary. Of course, that was during periods when I was not inflamed by Pauline Contini who lived up the block. She was an attractive woman of the world, being one whole grade ahead of me.

Lamarr Hall, Kenneth Bennett, and Tommy Kennally would come to my house on occasion for lunch, St. Thomas didn't have a lunch program, so you had to brown bag it, find a friend, or go to the corner restaurant for the marvelously salty, paper-thin hamburgers they served.

Every spring, the whole world would troop out to Riverside Park for an annual picnic. It must have been a dozen blocks away, but it seemed like a hike to the other side of the globe. We would scamper through the underbrush, swing on vines, angle for two-inch sunfish in the artificial lake, and make a great commotion in the woods.

I think often of Albert Mensi who left school after the eighth grade to work on the family farm. That was not an unusual thing in those days. High school was just beginning to be the norm for middle class America. Many considered my dad's six years of schooling more than adequate for those intending to get right to work.

Jimmy Harty was a short, feisty Irishman who delighted in picking fights with me. I was tall, thin, and altogether not inclined to mix it up. He kept after me until we finally had it out in the eighth grade. We fought to a draw in a combat that featured, as I recall, more hair-pulling than anything else.

The handsomest boy in the group was probably John Ronza who had the dark coloring and striking features of a Tyrone Power. Earline O'Hara was the brightest girl in class and my regular competitor for academic honors. I remember the pugnacious Allen Whitehead, the palely beautiful Julia Rohtert, and Geraldine Lucchesi, who turned out to be the owner of a cat I scooped off the street for a biology exhibit.

The names go on and on: Annette Dole, Francis Kowalski, Rose Cervetti, Betty John Moore, Joyce Coburn, Rosemary Nelson, and a dozen others whose faces linger in the mind without identification. Many names I recall are from classes just ahead of or behind mine; after a while I get them all mixed up.

Unfortunately, I won't make the reunion. I have to dismantle the Lincoln Park stage on the 28th. My distance from my Classmates is now a matter of geography and circumstance. It would be fun to see them again, to try to find the children I knew in grown up faces and bodies.

I look at those skinny kids up in front of the steps of the grade school and remember nothing of those days but the pure joy of being alive. Back when we lived and learned in a huge extended family, when each day spread out before us with endless possibilities, when we were primed for fun and a good 50 years away from nostalgia.

(9 October 1994)

Last year, some of the people with whom I grew up decided to hold a 50-year reunion. It was to mark our 1943 "graduation" from St. Thomas grade school in Memphis, Tennessee.

I didn't go last year, but wrote a column about my classmates and faxed it to them in time for the get-together. According to newspaper reports and letters I received after the party, it was such an enjoyable evening that they decided to make it an annual event.

Shortly afterward, I got a call from classmates John Coletta and Rose (Cervetti) Barton who must have learned a lot about Catholic guilt. They told me they would schedule this year's gathering whenever I could make it. With no room for evasion, I suggested September 17th and drove down to Memphis on that date to renew acquaintances.

Few family members are still living in Memphis: two nephews and one niece. My two sisters live elsewhere in Tennessee. I decided to make this one last trip to my childhood home and, while I was at it, to pay a final visit to Greenwood, Mississippi, where I spent most of my early summers.

I checked into a motel on Friday night and, after a good night's sleep, started the tour. I drove past our old homes on Lauderdale, Humber, Pond, and Marksman Streets. There were others I remembered, but those are the places I lived when attending St. Thomas.

I was stunned to find a vacant lot where the school once stood. It was hard to believe that a building which bulked so large in my memory could have occupied so small a space and have vanished so completely.

The convent was boarded up and, I guess, vacant. Even old St. Thomas Church was in bad shape. The roof of the bell tower has started to cave in. Mrs. Acerra's house, which stood between our home on Marksman Street and the school property, was in ruins; the roof collapsed along two-thirds of its length.

I didn't bother to get out of the car, except to take a picture of the church.

Just before noon, I headed south on Interstate 55 for Greenwood, about 90 minutes away. Driving down, I tried to remember some of the stops along the two Illinois Central Routes: Arkabutla, Senatobia, Tutwiler, Marks, Glendora, and Money: names that stay with you.

In Greenwood, I went straight to Oak Street, named for a line of huge trees which defined the block. My sister and I used to play for hours around their huge, exposed roots. I had been in Greenwood some twenty years before and found that time lay on everything like a light dust; nothing had changed.

But everything was missing this time: our house and all the others at that end of the block. Even the trees were gone. Had it not been for the street signs, I would not have believed I had come to the right place.

I drove to the cemetery and found the three graves I remembered along the back fence: Charles Chandler, Rose Martile, and David Wooten, Jr. My brother's headstone was the oldest, considerably weathered. His name and dates are not easily read.

Family fortunes weren't the best in those days; they bought sandstone instead of granite. The cruciform monument has crumbled in the rain. Strange to think he died so long ago, back in 1933. Water puddles on Aunt Rose's marker; grandad's headstone bulks above the others as he did in life.

I won't be back here again, so I take pictures. I also get snapshots of the business district, so oddly but clearly divided between black and white shops and patrons, and the muddy Yazoo River. On the way out of town, I paused for pictures of Kudzu vines, covering ground, trees, utility poles and wires, rather like a green, crenelated blanket.

I made a brief stab at locating Wooten, Mississippi, a village in DeSoto County, Mississippi, which was in the process of being deserted even in the thirties. All I found was the road which bore its name.

At the Bevico Country Club that Saturday night, I finally met my classmates, after a span of nearly half a century. Some were unmistakable; others had to be introduced. I was as unrecognizable as any.

Not everyone was there. About nine of the sixty are deceased and others have moved almost as far away as I have, although none of them moved north.

I apologized to Geraldine Lucchesi (an incident involving her cat which I won't go into), chatted with Earline O'Hara, my rival for scholastic honors, and gossiped over dinner with Velma Pretti, Ed Barbieri, Charles Brackey, Paul Acerra, Al and Elena Mensi, Nick Pesce, and Rose Marie Nelson.

After the meal, Bobby Moore, who looks very much like his father, asked someone to take a picture of him, me, and Isadore Johnson. As we stood there grinning for the camera, our arms about each other's shoulders and waists, I was suddenly overwhelmed by time.

How is it, I wondered, that the three of us, once so inseparable, whose lives were so tightly bound up with each other, have come together tonight as strangers?

I guess that's why I don't go to reunions. It's painful to be reminded how we drift away from those who are closest to us. How time, distance, and circumstance work at us, like rain in the Greenwood cemetery.

Words & Music

Two preoccupations came together in 1994.

(4 September 1994)

Along with passing the Crime Bill and messing up Health Care reform, Congress and the president took time to declare the month of September as Classical Music Month. As one who labors in that particular field of endeavor, I'd like to thank all of them for the honor.

It's not the same as money for concerts, you understand, but it's nice to have our leaders acknowledge that classical music is at least worth public notice.

Not that the public really noticed. After all, the proclamation didn't make major headlines — nothing does as long as O.J. Simpson awaits trial — so I thought I had better bring it up here just to be sure the news showed up somewhere in the press.

It's easy to downplay the whole thing. I seem to recall that pickles, among other items and events, are given a month of their own. Still, it's a step up from total indifference and we must be grateful for what we can get.

It's also good to know that a president who plays an earnest saxophone and admires Elvis Presley is sufficiently catholic in his tastes to give a boost to Bach, Beethoven, and their compatriots.

Not even Harry S. Truman, the only modern president who not only knew and loved classical music, but also regularly attended concerts by the National Symphony Orchestra, ever got around to giving classical music its own month. Or, if he did, I never heard about it and I'll bet you didn't either.

And it's nice to know that Bob Dole and Newt Gingrich went along with Clinton on this one. I'm not sure how they got around Jesse Helms, but it probably had something to do with the declaration being all talk and no money.

Americans have always had a problem with the notion that they should put tax dollars into something perceived as the province of the wealthy or the intelligentsia. Somehow, the silly notion has got around that classical music isn't for just plain folks. As one of the plain folks who loves the stuff, that makes me angry.

I grew up on the south side of Memphis, Tennessee, among people who had very little in the way of material goods. Yet we were all as conversant with the classics as we were with Roy Acuff and Ernie Tubbs.

That's because classical music was part of our common experience. It was on all the radio stations, especially on Sundays, and it was part of our education. Every Friday afternoon, all eight grades of St. Thomas School crowded into an upstairs hall for singing exercises with Sister Alphonse.

We spent some time singing Gregorian Chant (Now heading up popular music charts here and in Europe — go figure), hymns, popular music, and classical themes. In addition, many of us took music lessons and were inflicted on our classmates in recitals. The music was all "classical."

Also, in every Italian home, one could find wind-up Victrolas and thick, 78-rpm records of operatic arias by Enrico Caruso, Giuseppe Martinelli, Lily Pons, and Lawrence Tibbett.

Serious music wasn't exactly forced on us, but it was there along with everything else and most of us developed varying degrees of attachment to some pieces which could be termed "classical."

Kids don't have that kind of easy access to classical music anymore. It has become a victim of generational wars and the hunger for enormous profit from and for musical opportunists who don't want to lose their gold mines.

You see, much of the attraction of classical music comes from what one might call its complexity. Like real jazz, it rewards attentive listening and an ability to hear "into" the music. A lot is going on in a Beethoven symphony and the more you are able to hear, the deeper your pleasure becomes.

If kids remain stuck on a loud, monotonous base line with words shouted over guitars amplified beyond distortion, it's rather akin to spending their lives looking at comic books, rather than learning to read. It's fun, on a simplistic level, but it's a dead end.

The good stuff is in books without pictures and in music that admits of variety of form and expression. It's just not fair to permit youngsters to be shut out from either. They ought to hear real music in school and at home, if nowhere else.

Given a fair chance, every person will respond to deeper and richer musical experiences and that's just what you find in classical works. After all, something becomes a classic, not because it's dull and affected, but because generation after generation finds in it something important, even essential to life.

So, sometime during September, I hope you'll take time to give it a try. I defy you to hear the finale of Beethoven's sixth or ninth symphonies without responding to the music's power. Or play Ralph Vaughan Williams' "Serenade to Music" and really listen to the words.

Or try Liszt's piano solo, "Un Sospiro" (A Sigh), Copland's "Fanfare for the Common Man," Stravinsky's "Rite of Spring," Schumann's "Italian" Symphony, any overture by Wagner or Rossini, Tchaikovsky's "Romeo and Juliet," Bach's Toccata and Fugue in d, or his Passacaglia in c.

If you don't have these works on record, call WVIK at and we'll play them for you. It's worth the effort and, after all, this is classical music month.

(11 September 1994)

Not only is September Classical Music Month, as I noted last week, it is also Library Card Sign-Up Month. I guess I was so caught up in celebrating the one, I overlooked the other.

I am grateful to Pamela Goodes and Linda Wallace of the American Library Association for calling the omission to my attention. They mailed the information to me a week ago direct from the Association's Public Information Office in Chicago.

Lest you think that their letter was occasioned by a deep personal interest in my work, I should tell you that Pamela and Linda began their correspondence with "For Immediate Release" instead of "Dear Don."

Their communication may not have been personal (actually, it was sent to the WVIK Newsroom), but it was certainly thorough. Not only did they pass along the news about Library Card Sign-Up Month; they also included some public service spots for radio and a newspaper editorial, just in case I couldn't think of anything nice to say about library cards.

As it happens, I have a lot of nice things to say on the subject. Not perhaps, as inspired as their editorial which compares library cards to credit cards, to the enormous advantage of the former, but certainly more personal.

I don't remember just when I first got my public library card, but I am sure it was on the first day I was permitted to do so. Prior to that time, I had to content myself with rummaging through the St. Thomas Grade School library which had some reference works and a complete collection of Tom Swift books, but nowhere near as many volumes as the public library.

The library branch closest to my home was on McLemore Street. It wasn't a very imposing building: just a long rectangular room with book shelves lining three walls. As a matter of fact, it looked a lot like Rock Island's old Arrow Club, minus the bar and booths and with better lighting.

The McLemore library was at the far end of our neighborhood. At least, it seemed that way to me. It was a good hike from where I lived and my legs were much shorter in those days.

However, I made the trek every week and always took out the maximum number of books allowed — four. Nowadays they let you take out more than that, if you wish, but I always feel guilty doing it.

It took me about three days to read a week's allotment but, unless I was desperate for more information on a particular subject, I waited the full seven days before making another trip.

It may not have been an imposing building, but in that somewhat musty room I found the answers to my questions and discovered things I never knew existed. My interest in herpetology dates from finding books there by Raymond L. Ditmars; I explored the exotic world of opera, learned that stars were more than points of light, and chanced upon subjects which have held my interest into old age.

Then, one glorious day, I learned that my card was good, not only at the McLemore Branch, but at the main library in downtown Memphis. So, one fateful Saturday, I put my card in my pocket and hopped the Number 11 bus, got off on Main, and walked down to Front Street.

There it stood at the edge of the bluff overlooking the Mississippi River: The Memphis Main Library, a building which seemed to combine the noblest elements of castle, mansion, and prison. I had arrived at the Temple of Knowledge and held the key in my hand.

My elation gave way to disappointment when they told me I had to stay out of the adult section. I obeyed the rules for about a year but, being tall for my age, soon began to walk unchallenged into the place where the real books were kept. Like a master spy, I had penetrated the citadel and all its secrets lay open before me.

My next exciting discovery was that you didn't have to ask for books from the card catalogue; you could walk right back into the stacks and look for them yourself! To this day I can summon up those stacks, with dull light shining through the opaque, wire-reinforced, glass floors; book carts shuffling back and forth; and librarians murmuring in soft tones.

I had gone from the McLemore Branch to the Main Library, in much the same manner as one advances from high school to college. I could read anything I wanted — even though I sometimes had to endure the questioning looks of librarians who weren't sure I was old enough to cope with certain subjects, but who were too polite to say so.

And it cost me nothing! It was free! All I needed was a library card and that was free, too. True, it did take some spare change in my parents' taxes, but it was a pittance to pay for admission to all of human learning.

So, I guess Library Card Sign-Up deserves a month along with Classical Music. And it's a good idea to lump them into this September. Books and concerts; words and music — not a bad combination.

So, whether or not they print the library card vs. credit card editorial in the newspapers or run the radio spots at midnight, remember to celebrate this month by getting and using a library card.

But, please: don't take out more than four books at one time. Four seems an adequate number just now. After all, you'll also want to use your card to check out some classical records this month.

A Dandy(Lion) Lawn

Things can get out of hand. In recounting an effort to improve the appearance of our yard, I was pulled into a series of articles which ran on for years. I kept returning to the subject because it gave me a sneaky means of promoting WVIK's spring fund drive.

Shameless.

(15 May 1988)

This spring I made one of those irrational resolutions for which I am noted. You know the kind: "I'm going to take up tap dancing" or "I think I'll go on a diet."

I don't know what causes these wild impulses; probably a combination of rising sap and degenerating brain cells. But, again this April, I announced yet another futile resolve to my jaded family: "This year, I'm going to get rid of the dandelions."

That set off a two-week battle which is still raging. Armed with a dandelion weeder and assisted by a patient son, I have been prying hundreds of plants from the lawn, many of them dandelions.

The dandelion is a distinctive plant, with bright yellow blossoms which quickly turn into white puff¬balls which thoughtless children love to blow into the air. Its name is derived from the Latin, *dens leonis*, or "lion's tooth," a reference to the plant's saw-edged leaves. As you can see, I believe that it's important to know one's enemy.

So far, the struggle has been a series of short, furious encounters. I begin each attack with deft, graceful thrusts into the plant's root system. But, after the first 15 minutes or so, my style weakens and I end up on my knees, tearing wildly at anything green.

Every morning I survey the battlefield, and every morning there are more bright yellow flowers joining the fray. The dynamics of the contest is the rough equivalent of jungle warfare: the body count is impressive, but I have a sinking feeling that I will ultimately lose.

I have even skirted the Geneva Convention and practiced chemical warfare. The failure of this tactic convinces me that some Merry Andrew at the hardware store is slipping plant food into the chlordane.

But killing them isn't enough; they must be pursued into the grave. If and when you finally uproot the blasted things, you must get them into a garbage bag at once, for they quickly produce puffballs of seed, even as they are dying. And even when the poison does its work, the plant still has ample time to generate and disperse its seeds.

Bitter as the fight has been, I must confess that I have developed real respect for the enemy as well as a sneaking admiration. At the conclusion of each duel, I examine my foe from ground level. (This is easy to do as I am usually stretched out on the lawn trying to remember how my legs work.)

Examined from this vantage, the flowers are really rather pretty. In this posture (and condition), I have a hard time remembering exactly why they must be eliminated.

In fact, since violence hasn't worked, I am toying with another approach: pacifism. Even that ancient cold warrior, Ronald Reagan, was willing to sign a treaty with the Evil Empire. Maybe I ought to come to terms with *Taraxacum officinale.*

It might even be profitable. A friend recently told me of his interest in making dandelion wine. With his expertise and my crop, we could become the Gallo Brothers of the Midwest. My yard would be to dandelion wine what the Bordeaux region of France is to the Gallic kind.

Of course, there are other avenues of escape. I have obtained quotes from the folks at Astroturf and have looked into the advantages of green concrete.

But each of these alternatives amounts to surrender. I have sworn to rid my lawn of these tenacious growths and, barring a spinal collapse, I will.

Then, I think I'll take up tap dancing.

(7 May 1989)

Last week, I took-time off from work to participate in what has become, for me, a major observance: Dandelion Week.

Last year I wrote about this (you do save these things, don't you?) in a less than serious vein, but I assure you that this year I am not in a joking mood.

It was exactly two weeks ago today that the clouds finally remembered how to rain. Watching the two-plus inches accumulate, I sensed what was ahead and, sure enough, early Monday morning, the first yellow heads poked up through the barren soil. Dandelion Week was officially under way.

It's not a religious observance, understand, even though I spend much of the time on my knees, chanting, and muttering things which careless observers interpret as prayer. It is, rather, another step in the long, upward evolution of humankind, an attempt to assert a thinking creature's ascendancy over a short, green plant.

Philosophers don't talk about it very much, nor do religious leaders bring it up in sermons. That's because dealing with dandelions is a subject for tragedy, an event beyond considerations of truth or justice. It is a hero's quest against unimaginable odds, an attempt by mere mortals to overcome what many lawn specialists call "fate."

Recalling the words of our founding fathers, "Eternal vigilance is the price of a decent lawn," I prepared for the week with the determination and ceremony of a torero.

The dandelion spear was carefully cleaned and sharpened; heavy gloves laid by the door; and a careful survey made of the immediate vicinity. (I have given up the deep breathing exercises because this takes care of itself after about five minutes of work.)

It became evident at once that mine was a solitary undertaking. When I took the field Monday morning, I was the only one in the neighborhood so engaged. After three days of hard labor, with no other gladiator in sight, I understood that this was a battle I had to fight alone.

Remembering our experiences In Vietnam and Korea, I not only cleared my own lawn each day, but made pre-emptive strikes next door, creating a buffer zone across which, I hoped, few seeds would float. The score after day one was 74 dandelions, uprooted and bagged. The second day, I tore out 142, leaving them to wither on the sidewalk. On the third day, after clearing out some 200 plants, the mathematics of the situation came into focus: they were adding recruits and I was still alone.

Each day, I removed an ever-increasing number, now working in two shifts, with a reasonable break in between to give my back a chance to reform. After a week, my resolution was undimmed and the number of dandelions began to decline; I was winning at last.

By the 10th day, my lawn was clear; the buffer zone was in good shape; and I was still in fighting trim. But fate, in the form of WVIK's spring fund drive, intervened. I could no longer spare an hour or two each day for lawn work; raising money for public radio runs around the clock.

As, I left the house early last Wednesday, committed to staying till midnight, I saw my lawn occupied by the Yellow Horde. There must have been 300 in place, waiting for this moment.

As I walked to the car, I thought I heard smothered laughter and low sarcastic phrases about "the big gardener." They had simply waited me out and there was nothing I could do.

But that's the way it is in tragedy. You give it your best shot and accept the outcome, even though it can mean utter ruin or a yard full of dandelions.

(9 May 1993)

Four years ago, I wrote what I thought (and you hoped) would be my last column on the subject of dandelions. After all, how much can one find to say about a weed, especially one as common and ubiquitous as *Taraxacum officinale*?

To tell the truth, not much. The principal facts about them are well known: they are hardy, plentiful, and cunning. Every spring they dot my lawn and every spring I sally forth to dig them up. I uproot and collect piles of them each day and they appear in the same number and location the next. For all I know, they are even the same plants.

It is the most futile thing I have ever attempted and yet, each year I delude myself into thinking that they can be eradicated. It's rather like Congress cooperating with President Clinton: it seems possible, but somehow it never works out.

And it's not as if I can ignore them. When I leave the house in the morning, they pop up behind me as I pass along the walk. By the time I reach the street and look back, the lawn is a bright yellow, polka-dotted vista. "Okay!," I yell, "Just wait till this evening! I'll wipe out every last one of you!"

Their soft, flocculent laughter follows me into the car and lingers in my memory through the day. Come evening, when I am armed with the dandelion spear, they hunker into the tall grass and flatten out like green spiders. The golden swarm disperses into small units, which duck into tunnels as I approach and then gather in back of me to make faces and snide remarks.

Some people think I have gotten too deeply involved in this whole business, citing statements like the two previous paragraphs as proof that I have tipped over from husbandry into hysteria. But I am not one to be deterred by criticism. The struggle for a clean green lawn is botanical Holy War and I fight to the finish.

This doesn't mean that I don't have moments of doubt and fatigue. On one occasion, I even sought professional help — and not the kind you're thinking. I called in a lawn care specialist to give me an honest evaluation of my yard and its chances for dandelion-free perfection.

Oddly enough, he didn't just focus on the dandelions. He pointed out to me that I had one of the most extensive collections of exotic weeds he had ever seen. He circled around the yard, spotting varieties which seldom make the gardening books. I could tell he was impressed. "You don't often find this much moss in an average yard, either," he added.

I began to suspect that he was setting me up for a series of expensive treatments; that he planned to enrich himself transforming my yard into a Kentish dream. But I may have misjudged him. His advice was forthright and honest. For, unless he was also a dealer in concrete and green paint, I don't see how he could have profited from his suggestions.

A friend tells me that I have been going at it the wrong way. He controls dandelions in a devastatingly direct manner: he collects them when they are small and tender and incorporates them into salads. Apparently when the plants find out you will not only pick them but eat them as well, they pick up and move into the neighbor's yard.

This, by the way, is where they gather to regroup after one of my attacks. My son, who lives next door, has a much more relaxed view of lawn care than I. He will mow his yard from time to time but, otherwise, takes a *laissez faire* attitude toward its composition.

So, even as I am weeding them out, scouts from my son's lawn are being sent in to replace them. I went around to the far side of his house last week, and found a gaggle of monster dandelion plants, grown huge and arrogant in the safety of his indifference, including one which I am pretty sure is the Ur-Dandelion, the one from which all others are descended. I dug at them until my back gave out (something which is happening rather more quickly these days — probably the result of prolonged exposure to dandelion pollen) and left a heap of uprooted tribal elders in a pile by his basement window.

By now they have probably replanted themselves and are recruiting reckless young rootlings to make midnight forays into my yard.

The whole thing seems so hopeless. Five years ago I set out to eliminate dandelions from my property and, thus far, have never seen a warm day in which several of them are not thumbing their noses at me from some corner of the yard. "Zero Tolerance" may work in society's war against drugs and violence, but it hasn't done a thing to improve my lawn. No matter how vigorously I pursue my strategies, the dandelions survive; they persist; they thrive.

I wouldn't council the police to abandon their efforts to control crime just because similar measures fail in the plant kingdom. After all, drug dealers maybe as persistent as dandelions, but dandelions are a whole lot smarter.

(4 May 1997)

It's been fully three years since I last wrote about dandelions, promising that it would be my final word on the subject. Grateful readers mailed their thanks to the editor along with a variety of flattering comments.

(One, in particular, expressed the fervent hope that she would soon "see the back" of me. The poor woman had obviously confused me with Mel Gibson.)

It was a promise that I fully intended to keep, but this season has gotten off to a bad start, putting me under a lot of pressure. Part of it has to do with WVIK's spring fund drive, but much of it flows from the devious behavior of these insidious plants.

It seems the dandelions got mixed up this year. Their usual practice is to wait until the on-air drive starts in late April and then pop up to litter my yard with puffballs, knowing I would be too busy to do anything about it.

Imagine their surprise when this year's campaign was pushed back a week. As I ventured into the yard 10 days ago, armed with my dandelion spear, you could almost hear tiny cries of "Oops!" on all sides. Grabbing Old Mulchmaker, I marched through the yard, hacking and bagging one advance scout after another. Some pulled themselves back into the ground (They can do that, you know) until later in the day, thinking that surely I would go back to work.

But I fooled them. I walked to the driveway, got in my car, and slammed the door. A moment later, I jumped out, raced back, and caught a dozen of them stretching and laughing.

It was a great feeling to be in command of the field, but I knew that it was only a temporary victory. Sooner or later, the Big Weed at Dandelion GHQ would find a way to turn the tide.

In fact, they already have it sorted out. I imagine that one of them tuned in 90.3 FM and got the right schedule.

Within 24 hours, every last *Taraxacum officinate* had been advised and a new plan of attack worked out. The great bulk of them laid low until the fund drive began this past Thursday.

Every morning since, as I have raced out of the house to get to the station on time, dozens would be lined up, thumbing their noses at me (They have noses, too). They know I can do nothing more than mutter imprecations and make rude gestures at them.

The thin sound of their lemony laughter is grating. By the time I get on the air, the desperation shows in my voice. Casual listeners think it has something to do with trying to meet our formidable goal ($150,000), but that's an incidental concern.

I know that, while I am chattering away at WVIK, they are swaggering about the lawn, toasting each other and chortling as they spread millions of seeds in the time it takes me to raise a handful of pledges.

They call out to dandelions in other yards, inviting them to come over and bring their hairy friends with them. By the time the fund drive finishes this Wednesday, it'll take napalm just to find where the dog's chain is anchored.

It's not only rough on me; it's also a matter of deep concern to Bernadette. For some reason, she doesn't like to have me talk to strangers about all this. They tend to stare and edge away, but that's because they understand the enormity of my problem.

She occasionally comes out in the yard to watch me. It's not that she enjoys the unequal contest (I never win), but because she knows that, as my energy flags, my temper rises. After a few minutes of selective slaughter, my eyes dim, my back cramps into a permanent stoop, and I begin to swing wildly at anything yellow.

She has a blind attachment to her tulips and turns the hose on me when I go after the golden ones.

I realize that I should take this whole business less seriously. Any reputable philosopher will tell you that dandelions are the earth's primary species and it is useless trying to deny them their dominant role in the solar system.

It's rather like King Canute ordering back a saffron tide, only to have the yellow wave engulf him.

Better that I choose some other, more rational aim in this life. A goal that is nobler, less violent, more worthy of my exertions. An objective which, because of its intrinsic value, will draw others to the cause.

The number to call is 794-7500.

(1 May 1994)

The letters generated by this column — apart from demands that it be stopped forthwith — make up in enthusiasm what they lack in number. The most recent correspondence was an exhortation, replete with poetic quotations, to enjoy spring. It also included a reminder that it is time to deal with dandelions again.

I like to think I have grown beyond such things. While it is true that I have expended a fair amount of energy (and a comparable quantity of ink) in the past, trying to eradicate the botanical Yellow Menace, I have mellowed to a point at which I am now ready to coexist with the enemy.

Of course, I could be Serbian about it: declare a truce, only to attack once more. But the fact is that I am honestly tired of trying to make my lawn conform to some Better Homes and Garden ideal. No matter what I do to it, my yard will never come up to the standards set by the master gardeners of Kent, so I'm through trying.

What I'll do instead is apply American entrepreneurial imagination to the problem and turn my liability into an asset. If I can't transform my lawn into a putting green, why not turn it into a Weed Museum?

I could put a fence around the place, set up a turnstile, and charge curious citizens a modest sum to see a collection of botanical grotesqueries they could not match without trekking through a dozen museums. One quick turn about the place would bring them face to face with a gardener's worst nightmares, safely (and permanently) rooted in one place.

Tasteful signs along area highways would advise tourists of a rare opportunity to examine, in one convenient stop, the legendary despoilers of the suburban dream. Of course, 1 would have to take the trouble of putting up little signs identifying each species, in particular the ones from Mars, but that's a lot easier than trying to dig them out.

And don't think I'm just in this for the money. There are important environmental concerns at stake. At a time when people are bulldozing acres of rare species in the Amazonian Jungle and eradicating the old-growth forests in the Pacific Northwest, shouldn't we be doing something to preserve the really ugly plants of the Midwest?

I'm not sure where you stand on the question, but l am ready to turn in my dandelion spear and start cashing in. Not only does Weed Preservation have a noble, humanitarian ring to it, it involves a lot less work. In fact, no work at all. The time I used to spend grubbing in the yard can now be spent lolling in a hammock, listening to the crabgrass spread.

Those thick, stubbly plants with tough hides and roots into infinity which routinely blunt my shears will now be permitted to reach their full potential. They usually grow about six inches in one week; a summer without trimming may enable them to reach gargantuan proportions. In fact, they may even be a species of tree; I'm not very good at Taxonomy.

My plans include the installation of a small research unit to house two or three experimental botanists. Surely there is grant money available to study the Bermuda Triangle of the plant world. I cannot be the only person who wonders why grasses planted in my yard vanish without a trace.

There is also the puzzling phenomenon I call the Mutant Attractor. Why do these strange life forms gather in my yard and not in others? Is some exotic mineral located here which grows them? Is there, perhaps, a radioactive source underground which turns grass into hairy, broadleaf, pod-producing monsters?

Was my yard, in fact, the inspiration for "Little Shop of Horrors?"

As you can tell, I've thought about the subject a lot; perhaps too much. But one can spend only so many hours in idle speculation; sooner or later, issues must be addressed and answers found. After a winter of deliberation, it is time for action.

There are two choices before me: to put on the gloves, take up the dandelion spear, and return to the attack; or to turn adversity into profit while pushing back the frontiers of botanical knowledge.

On the one hand, lie hours of stooping, weeding, and the certainty of failure. On the other, the possibility for enhanced income, scientific advancement, and a statue in the Botanical Center.

Which would you choose?

I agree. The Wooten Weed Museum will open just as soon as I figure out how to take tickets without getting out of the hammock.

Gracie, Swanie, God

Meditations in church.

(21 November 1993)

About 25 of us met at Dubuque last Tuesday morning: all members of one of those extended Iowa families with three or four generations of relatives scattered all over the country.

I was admitted to this remarkable group by virtue of my marriage to Bernadette. Wootens tend to be solitary creatures, so it took me awhile to loosen up and join in the fun. It really wasn't difficult; there is always someone available in that diverse but close-knit family to make an in-law feel at home.

We met at the Marian Hall Chapel of the Sisters of Charity of the Blessed Virgin Mary, familiarly known as the BVMs. We had come to the Mount Carmel motherhouse to say goodbye to Grace Ellen Brecht, who entered the congregation in 1935 and died in its service last weekend.

The administrator remarked that it was unusual to have so many family members present at a funeral. She told me that often there are few relatives living close enough to attend and that sometimes the sister is the last surviving member of her family.

The chapel was filled with surviving sisters, a number of them in wheelchairs. The heads which were not covered by the old-fashioned veil were mostly white. A goodly number of the sisters have retired to the motherhouse to end their service where it had begun in the novitiate many years ago.

Looking around the chapel, one could see the real strength of the Catholic Church: its women. Bishops and priests may have power and authority, but it has been the nuns who put a human face on it. They are the ones who have done the work and they are the ones we remember with most affection.

Gracie was the youngest of eight siblings, born across a span of a generation to William and Grace Ellen Abbe Brecht. Bernadette's mother, Hildred, was the oldest and Bernadette and Gracie were born not too many years apart. Gracie visited with us every summer, dividing her vacation time between our home and her brother Paul's in Moline.

Two summers ago, she went out east to attend her ailing sister, Laurene. This last summer saw the onset of the cancer which was to bring her life to an abrupt halt. We drove up to see her before Bernadette's surgery; we sensed it would be the last time.

Gracie's first assignments were in teaching. This was not work for which she felt well suited, but in 1937 nuns were expected to staff Catholic schools, so that's what she did. Finally, in 1968, she was able to take up nursing, the profession she loved, and stayed at until she became a patient herself about nine months ago.

The family assembled behind the screen of stained glass figures that stood behind the altar. We renewed acquaintances, met Gracie's classmates and friends, and paid our personal respects at the casket which stood to one side. The vows she had taken 58 years ago were neatly typed and displayed on the lower half of the casket.

We joined in the procession behind the casket into the chapel proper for the funeral mass. The choir sat behind us and their quavering soprano voices led the congregation in responses and hymns.

Bernadette showed me Gracie's parting gift to her: a rosary and the ring which had been placed on her finger all those years ago, marking her as a bride of Christ, married to poverty, chastity, and obedience.

During the sermon, the priest who celebrated mass mentioned, in an aside, that the meetings of the U.S. Catholic bishops were being televised on cable and that it would be rewarding for all of us to tune in. Ever the heretic, I thought that the sight and sounds of Marian Hail that day would be the more edifying experience.

When Mass was over, the casket was wheeled out of the chapel. Family members followed and, after us, the choir. The procession went down the hallway, through the front door, to the waiting hearse.

As the procession formed, the members of the choir started singing a hymn which obviously had deep meaning for them, "Mother of Mount Carmel." Where they had sung in unison before, their voices now blossomed into harmony. Where the responses in the mass had not always been together or in perfect pitch, now they sang with assurance and control.

The undertaker slid the casket into the hearse as the long procession formed into a semi-circle in front of Marian Hall. The hymn grew in volume. Then, the hearse drew away from us and started its solitary journey to the cemetery on the far side of the Mount Carmel property.

I could not help but think, at that moment, of Gracie leaving her delightful family at the age of 18 to enter the convent. In leaving that circle of support, she must have felt very much isolated. She was going to another life, one amid strangers, with faith and hope as her only guides.

In that new family she would find a love and support not less warm and supportive than her family's, but she was terribly alone at the beginning. Alone, once more, she left us standing and singing atop Mount Carmel.

> *"Mother of Mount Carmel, hear.*
> *Shades of night are falling, night is near."*

(20 March 2005)

Every other person in the Quad-Cities seems to have shown up for the Rev. Richard A. Swanson's wake, funeral, or memorial service this week. I doubt that I shall ever see so many people in a church again.

Swanie was a special person; but then, you probably know that from first-hand experience. His life impacted thousands. Others have written and talked about him this week, so there is little point in repeating stories of his limitless generosity and tireless service.

So, let me dwell instead on a long-standing joke.

When Bernadette and I spoke briefly with Lorian Swanson last Monday, I had only one question: "Of what religion was he when he died?"

All of us have kidded Swanie about his involvement in so many different religions. He was a one-man ecumenical movement. I told

Lorian I fully expected him to be ushered into the next life — if there is one — by Martin Luther, St. Francis, St. Teresa, Moses, Buddha, Mohammed, Lao-Tse, and Jesus; not necessarily in that order.

She laughed and said that just two days before his sudden death, he announced that he was a Quaker. So William Penn probably joined the celestial queue, as well.

It is this very quality in Swanie that I prized so highly. He was that rarity in religion: a genuinely tolerant person. For most people, commitment to a particular religion tends to throw up a wall against others.

After all, what we choose to believe — if we truly believe it — carries with it the compelling idea that other approaches to god are either wrong or insufficient. Those who believe with us help to fortify that conviction, in large measure to justify themselves.

Consoled and strengthened by those who think with us, it's only natural to settle into strong orthodoxies and to regard those outside the fold as heretics or potential converts.

In a wholly secular society, one which neither encourages nor discourages religion, such convictions and behaviors need not be a problem. But once let a country tilt toward a theocracy and all sorts of abuses become possible. You don't have to look very far in this world to find them.

In his New York Times' review of Rev. Robert Drinan's new book "Can God and Caesar Coexist?" John T. Noonan, Jr. cites James Madison's three arguments for the free exercise of faith in a religion-neutral state:

"(1) Nothing equips the state to decide theological disputes or guide citizens to salvation; (2) religious persecution created hypocrites and bigots, and religious establishments created a corrupt clergy; (3) an individual's obligation to the Creator transcends any duty to the state." He added, "For Christians, force is repudiated by every page of the gospels."

Drinan, a Jesuit who served a short period in the U. S. House of Representatives, understands the pressures either to resist a state religion or to embrace it. The balance between religious conviction and religious liberty is difficult to maintain — assuming that's what you want to do.

To suggest that another's path to the Divine is just as valid or effective as your own is, to the mind of a convinced Jew, Christian, Muslim, etc., heresy, and cause for being cast forth from the fellowship.

The fact that Swanie was tolerant and semi-involved in other religions, did not undercut the strength of his own convictions or his devotion to his own church. I think he just accepted that the practice of virtue does not depend on adherence to any particular orthodoxy.

That's the way the early Christians appear to have been: more concerned with trying to follow Jesus' example rather than insisting that everyone had to sign onto a theological constitution. It was some of the leaders who demanded — and ultimately got — a set of codified beliefs to which everyone had to conform or be excommunicated.

That's still the way it goes today. The great faiths are splintered into competing — and, often, warring — camps which admit no quarter. Pastor, rabbi, mullah: all are power positions which can corrupt the people who occupy them. Indeed, all professions or leadership roles can be viewed as power positions. And power is not easily yielded.

But Swanie wasn't interested in those games. He was interested in people. He met them on their own terms, listened, and helped. If that help meant stretching what we might call "traditional" bounds, then that's what he did.

"Judge not, lest ye be judged." That was scripture Swanie took to heart; which is why so many people took him to theirs.

(6 December 1992)

What with weddings, funerals, masses, prayer meetings, and memorials, I have spent a fair amount of time in church over the past few months. As diverse as the occasions were which drew me to these services, I found one constant in them all: the Lord's Prayer.

At some point in every ceremony, joyous or sad, the congregation is invited to join in a group recitation and, without giving the matter much thought, everybody chimes in.

I know it is the basic prayer in Christianity, the one we are instructed to use, but I have always considered it one or the most dangerous choices of words you can use in addressing God.

That notion first struck me as a child. By the time I was in the seventh or eighth grade, the daily recitation of the Lord's Prayer was strictly routine, delivered by rote whenever the occasion arose. But looking at the words in print one day, I was suddenly chilled to realize what I had been saying.

It's a phrase which comes a little more than halfway through: "Forgive us our trespasses as we forgive those who trespass against us." That's a breathtaking thought: asking God to forgive us only to the extent that we forgive those who have done us harm. In reciting that prayer, a person does not ask for mercy, but for a very grim, even-handed justice.

That ranks right up there with "Love your enemies. Do good to those who hate you." It is the core of Christianity, a giant step beyond the beliefs of the Essenes, the radical notion which truly sets Christianity apart.

It is also the most universally ignored precept in all of religion. How could any person who recites that prayer ever fight with another? How could Catholic Irish bomb Protestant English? How could fundamentalist Baptists fall into bitter, warring factions? How could Christian athletes blindside an opposing quarterback?

When you get right down to it, that kind of attitude could dry up the dog-eat-dog competition that drives bottom-line business, reduce political campaigns to genteel discussions, and prompt pro-choice and pro-life groups to help each other distribute leaflets.

How is it that so many people continue to ask for such a bleak contract with God? Are they hypocrites or merely forgetful? Or do they, perhaps, assume that God is only half-listening?

It's not for me to judge, but I imagine that the doggerel verse by that popular poet, Anon, sums things up rather neatly:

"A Christian is a man who asks forgiveness on a Sunday.
For what he did on Saturday and is going to do on Monday."

Let's face it: the standard set in the Lord's Prayer is one that precious few of us are ever going to live up to. It was George Bernard Shaw who cited Christianity as a wonderful idea and thought it a pity that it had never really been tried.

That's the way religion has fared in the world, gradually temporizing and adjusting to the way people behave. That's not to say that strict codes of conduct are not preached and, in some churches and nations, ruthlessly enforced. But in such cases there is usually a consensus on conduct to begin with. The really tough rule just isn't brought into sharp focus.

There are any number of dodges: "Love the sinner, hate the sin" is the most common. But the usual result is that the two get all mixed up in practice. It's hard to punish a sin without inflicting at least some discomfort on the sinner. What is a prayful person to do?

I don't know. One certainly can't advocate a rephrasing of the Lord's Prayer; after all, the instructions in its form and usage were fairly specific. And not even the best Washington lawyer can interpret its language to mean something less Draconian.

I'm no help in the matter. I know full well what I'm saying, yet it's difficult to abstain from prayer when all about me are going at it full throttle. I've learned to live with inconsistency and I guess you'll have to do the same.

Either that, or start mumbling.

"Air You Jeff?"

Among hundreds of stories about the people I have known, these two involving Jeff Holtz deserve to stand alone.

(28 April 1996)

They are Jeff's stories, but I'm going to tell them.

Of course, it would be better coming from Jeff. He holds you with his eyes, paces carefully, gestures, and exercises that sonorous voice to perfection. But none of that comes across in print, so we'll just make do with this.

Jeff is Jeff Holtz. He came up yesterday to help raise pledges during WVIK's spring drive. His was the very first voice to utter our call letters, back some 34 years ago when WVIK first went on the air as a 10-watt student station.

Jeff came back to the station in the eighties, after it had been transformed into a major National Public Radio outlet, covering an 80-mile sweep across eastern Iowa and northwestern Illinois.

He spent three years as our overnight announcer, then moved on to a position as music director of WIUM in Macomb. He still provides a weekly program of folk music which we carry on Saturday nights, so our paths cross from time to time.

One Saturday, Jeff and I were talking to Laura Lane, director of the NOVA Singers. We were swapping stories about memorable choral performances when Jeff provided the capper.

It happened back in 1965 when Jeff was returning from a six-month training stint with the National Guard. He got off the bus in downtown Rock Island in a driving rain and hustled over to WHBF-TV, where he had worked for a while as cameraman.

Jeff hit town shortly before the crest of the '65 flood arrived. There was a flurry of activity at all points along the river and John Ravencroft, the channel four anchorman, was setting out to get some footage.

Jeff offered to go along to haul equipment. This was before today's light portable video machines. Ravencroft wanted some sound, so they had to cart the large, clunky camera WHBF-TV used for that purpose.

They packed up the camera and all the extension cords they could find (no battery operation for this monster) and set off for the sandbagging operation behind the Farmall Plant in Rock Island.

They got there at about the same time as the Augustana Choir. The Augie students had just returned from their annual concert tour and had taken a short hour to wolf down dinner before hurrying out to help.

As the students formed a sandbag line, Jeff and John found a place to plug in one of the extensions and started linking them together so that they could position the camera along the levee wall.

There wasn't much light — just some isolated sources placed at irregular intervals, but John thought they had enough to get something on film.

The conditions were wretched for that kind of work: muddy underfoot, minimum light, and driving rain. Still, the camera light came on, so they had some power and they started to film.

And then, the choir began to sing.

Bone-tired after their long trip, operating on a hasty meal, and doing back-breaking work in a downpour, the youngsters started singing Schubert's "Ave Maria."

It was a magical moment. The simple, familiar prayer in Schubert's sublime setting, rising in that place under those conditions, moved Jeff in a way he cannot recount without his voice breaking.

Ravencroft, never at a loss for words, was speechless. But he knew a great story when he saw and heard it and focused on the choir.

They shot about 800 feet of film as the youngsters continued to work and sing. Jeff forgot all about the rain and he speculates that Ravencroft had visions of network exposure, perhaps a Peabody Award.

They went back to the station and threaded the film up to be developed and sat down to await the result of their night's toil.

At this point, Laura and I broke in with the same question: "Where is that film?" I was especially puzzled, because I put together a documentary on the flood, using WHBF's footage as its basis and had never seen it.

"You remember that old camera?" he asked. "It used to cut in and out on occasion and that night it failed completely. The light signaled that it was on, but not one foot of film was exposed." The magical moment was lost.

Ravencroft was noted for his temper and Jeff thought it lucky that he didn't break up the newsroom that night. He had complained about the camera repeatedly but could never squeeze enough money out of the station to have it replaced.

John announced that he would stay at the station until the news director came in. He wanted to tell him what his parsimony had cost. Jeff tried to calm him down for an hour before finally giving up and going home.

No one knows what Ravencroft said that morning, but he left the station shortly after for a job in Chicago. And the camera stayed in service until I quit in 1971.

So that night cannot be relived except in Jeff's words. But it lives for him and you can visualize that remarkable scene as it unfolds in his words.

Here's another one from about 20 years later.

Jeff stopped in a tavern along Moline's Seventh Avenue one afternoon and got to talking to the bartender about music. The only other person in the place was a rather unkempt individual in an undershirt and scruffy trousers.

The man moved to the bar, drawn by their conversation. He broke into their exchange by asking Jeff what kind of music he liked. Jeff thought at first the guy wanted to pick a fight. But he responded honestly that he enjoyed all kinds of music but that he made a minor league living playing classical music, so he guessed that was his favorite.

At that, the man's eyes lit up and he asked, "Air you Jeff?"

It turned out that the man was down and out, living alone in a small room, with no job and no prospects. As you might imagine, there was little pleasure in his life, with one exception: a miniature, battery-powered radio that barely worked.

He couldn't pick up anything he liked by turning it on in his room; he had to take it out in the park, which he did late at night.

What he listened to was Jeff's overnight program of classical music, "Nocturne."

Working at a classical music station, we hear a lot of stories like that. There is something special about great music at night, whether sung on a rain-soaked levee or picked up on a failing transistor.

You may be toiling in a difficult undertaking, dreading the dawn, wanting companionship, or simply staring at a blank space in your life. When not much else serves your need, music can and will.

Great music strengthens, consoles, reaffirms, and delights. It's made a difference in many lives: in Jeff's, in mine, and, I hope, in yours.

That fact is why we're working in public radio.

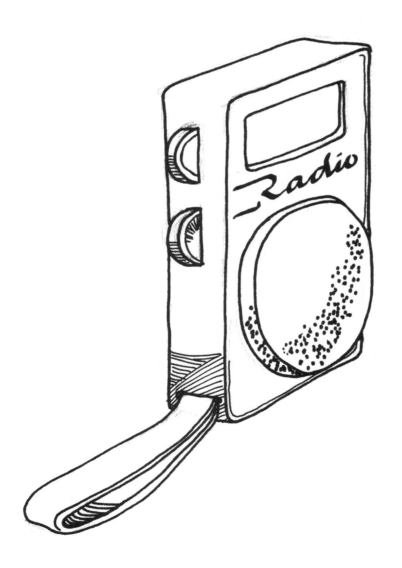

Politics

Once you join the circus, the greasepaint seeps into your blood. Much the same thing happens in politics. It just isn't as funny.

(4 April 2004)

You might be surprised to discover that I am a card-carrying member of the Republican Party — a platinum member, no less — and I have the card to prove it.

I'm not sure how I achieved membership so easily. I haven't been in contact with any party officials, nor have I sent them money. But they seem to be trusting souls and have mailed me a card to flash at conservative gatherings, along with an invoice for 2004 dues.

While party philosophers are solidly against the graduated income tax, they have given me a range of membership prices from which to choose. We Republicans are flexible in such matters.

Not only that, but I have received earnest solicitations to go door-to-door to urge like-minded citizens to register to vote so that they can support the Bush-Cheney team in November. This presumes that Cheney will not be dropped in favor of a more lifelike running mate.

And don't think this is something new. President Reagan sent me a photograph of himself and Nancy when he was in office, not once, but twice, along with a personal invitation to attend a private leadership meeting he was scheduling for special friends.

Unfortunately, I didn't have the dough at hand to take him up on this unique opportunity. I forget whether the amount was $2,500, $25,000, or $125,000. I remember the 25 and several zeroes. It was clearly beyond my means. Still, it was the thought that counted.

Nor did it stop there. George the First also sent me a picture of himself and Barbara, waving cheerfully as they embarked on some kind of journey. I kept that on my desk for quite a while. He also invited me to a gathering of his major supporters, but the price tag was, once again, a bit hefty.

I can't be sure about the earlier invitations, but I think the latest was the result of my joining the American Heritage Society at the bargain-basement price of $25.00. I believe that this expression of interest opened the door to a broad range of Republican-related organizations and fellow travelers.

For example, I just got a letter from Judicial Watch which is continuing its campaign to bankrupt the Clintons through an interminable series of lawsuits. I gather from reading their literature that their passion in the matter remains undimmed, almost four years after the president left office.

There's something touching about that. They still pursue their ideals, even though it's hard to understand why.

Those who are convinced of a link between Republican organizations and certain religious groups will not be surprised to learn that I have been getting mailings urging me to do strange things, like putting on a paper sandal and returning it in the mail to secure financial blessings.

The sandal was followed by a prayer mat (I thought that was a Muslim practice) and the number "three" in felt, all of which were to be returned, preferably with a donation, to realize untold blessings, among them a steep increase in cash flow. (Enough to afford a presidential briefing?)

All that for $25.00 to the American Heritage Foundation. All I wanted was a peek into the thinking of the party's philosophers, but I got so much more. Trouble is, now they want another twenty-five bucks. They also sent me a splendid plastic membership card, in anticipation of my continued involvement. They seem pretty sure of themselves.

But please don't think I have been neglected by the Democrats. Nancy Pelosi urges me to join the campaign to elect a Democratic Congress with a small — or sizable — donation. She also included a card.

Hillary Clinton is also interested in my participation in her fundraising activities. Bill would like my continued support for his library (I bought a brick for the sidewalk some time ago). Various candidates from both parties have solicited my financial support for their individual campaigns. And, of course, various friends in office remember me at election time. Having been through the mill myself, I try to help out.

Jimmy Carter has been my most consistent correspondent. I get a Christmas card every year from him and Rosalyn. On occasion, he includes newsletters about his ongoing campaigns in Africa to eradicate Guinea Worm Disease and AIDS. He also provides candid assessments of current African leaders. On that score, I get better information from him than from the media.

His last letter contained a fascinating bit of news. In one African country, a number of doctors from Cuba had been dispatched by Castro to aid Carter in his work. That collaboration of communists and capitalists finally brought out my checkbook.

It is truly amazing to find oneself on the receiving end of so many opportunities to join the ranks of both major parties. As well as the independents. The Greens have sent similar invitations, but I fear my response to them has been short and uncivil. Nothing about them; it's all about Nader.

I've even heard from a socialist candidate in Vermont. And, of course, there are people in Nigeria who could use my help in collecting some truly fabulous sums of money, for which service they will reward me handsomely.

I guess once you send money to one group, the word gets out. Rather like Depression Days when, after being fed, hoboes marked a "soft touch" sign on your fence to alert fellow panhandlers.

(6 March 1988)

Okay, I'll admit it: I'm hooked. I thought I could give it up after an eight-year addiction, but I have to confess that it's a habit which may take years of counseling to overcome. Personally, I think I'm beyond a cure.

I'm a legislative junkie.

It started when I served in the Illinois senate. The debates weren't tedious; they were fascinating. Committees weren't boring; they were enlightening. Sure, it was tiring, and some sessions went on at mind-numbing length, but I found something to enjoy at every moment.

In the Legislature, you must deal with real issues and you must make a decision. You know going in that, no matter how carefully you examine the issue and how carefully you draw a bill, you may wind up doing as much harm as good.

So you question some more; you argue with friends and foes; you solicit opinions and testimony; you sample views informed and uninformed; you dodge and pause and quibble and, finally, you decide.

There is simply nothing like it. It is the noblest and most exasperating job the mind of man has yet devised and it is habit-forming.

In former times, when the voters threw you out, you had no choice but to quit cold turkey. But now there's C-Span on cable TV, with gavel-to-gavel coverage of both houses of Congress, which militates against a cure for weak-willed fellows such as I.

I recently watched Senator Byrd of West Virginia on the Senate floor outlining the schedule for the next day. It took an hour of exquisite, carefully worded detail and I drank in every moment. It was then that my family started talking about getting professional help for me.

When Byrd sent the sergeant-at-arms out to arrest senators dodging a filibuster, it was more exciting than "Miami Vice." (Of course, most anything is more exciting than "Miami Vice.")

But a case can be made for this unseemly obsession. Legislative conduct may look and sound like an overdrawn, verbal ballet, replete with antique language and outdated conventions. The process may seem unending and unproductive. But I contend that the heart of a democracy beats in its legislative bodies and nowhere else.

Democracy is not dependent on any individual; not the president; not even the young blithely giving their lives in foreign lands (young men have died desperately for many modes of government, good and bad); not the selfless community benefactor (such are the salt of the earth, but not necessarily the savor of democracy).

No. What citizens have lived and died for is that quaint meeting of ordinary people charged with making the law. They must make decisions, even though they cannot agree on anything, representing, as they do, the most diverse collection of individuals on the face of the earth.

The rules are elaborate to insure fairness. The manner is overly polite to make it possible to keep talking after agonizing fights. The aim is to accomplish the impossible: making laws which are just.

Legislative work is never a wholly satisfying endeavor. A person never accomplishes exactly what he or she thinks is right. But that's as it should be. Democracy fails if one group completely dominates another on any point, so total victory is always denied, even to those who are convinced that they are on the side of the angels.

It's not getting the job done which makes legislative service addictive; it's the process itself: the give and take among people who represent contradictory interests and constituencies; the forging of a kind of fellowship where fellowship would seem to be impossible.

It is the crucible in which democracy is forged anew, day after day, session after session. It is not the hope of our nation; it is the fact of our nationhood.

Even at the distant remove of television, it remains one of the most compelling experiences I have ever known and I don't think I'll ever lose a taste for it.

The Crazy Eight: Don Wooten, Vivian Hickey, Ken Buzbee, Bill Morris, Dawn Clark Netsch, Terry Bruce, Vince DeMuszio, Jerry Joyce

The Crazy Eight

During my eight years in Springfield, a lot of my energy was devoted to keeping the Crazy Eight together, summoning members to almost nightly meetings to discuss bills and exchange information. We came from all parts of the state and fairly represented its divergent views. It was the most energetic, intelligent, and insightful group of people I have ever worked with.

(2 May 2004)

Vince Demuzio was laid to rest in Carlinville, Illinois, yesterday. He was the last of the "Crazy Eight" to leave the senate, as he was, in a sense, the last to join the group.

I know that any reference to a group of Illinois senators active in the 70s is going to be of little interest to the general reader, but it was a special time in Illinois politics and a special group of people. Not special because I was a member, but because of the make-up of the group and the extraordinary talents its members brought to the legislative process.

Saying that Vince was last in and last out needs some explaining. The original, five-member group was organized informally at a meeting of newly-elected senators at a late 1972 orientation meeting.

I had read in state newspapers of several promising Democratic candidates that year (I was not among them). I looked up those who survived the election and suggested that we ought to form some kind of informal gathering to help each other understand the legislative process.

Ken Buzbee of Carbondale said that's exactly what he was thinking and Betty Ann Keegan of Rockford immediately agreed. Standing with us was Terry Bruce of Olney who had been in the senate for two years and had been given a very rough time there for a variety of reasons — worth discussing in another context some time. He wanted in and we welcomed the experience he would bring.

Then Keegan suggested that we ought also to invite Dawn Clark Netsch of Chicago. I objected to anyone from Chicago, lest that person provide a pipe back to City Hall. Keegan assured me that Dawn was one of those notorious North Shore liberals and not in Mayor Daley's organization.

The first thing we decided was that we should seek committee assignments that would place at least one of us on every committee. Then, we would meet every evening to go over testimony, so that all would have a clear picture of what was in process.

We agreed early on that we were in no way obliged to vote with one another — and some of our most spirited fights in the future were between members. But the camaraderie forged in that daily exchange of honest information kept us together and talking for years.

We suffered a blow when Betty Ann Keegan died a year after being elected. She developed a dry cough during that initial orientation meeting, the first symptom of the cancer that would take her life.

But Rockford was supplied with a number of truly impressive, politically active women and they sent a great replacement, Vivian Hickey. Our daily meetings did not go unnoticed and we were challenged again and again in caucus about our "mini-caucus." I explained "the

Democratic Study Group" so often that I began to suspect my colleagues weren't listening.

We were the products of the 1972 election, the year that Dan Walker was elected governor. Only one of the group had a relationship with Walker, the rest ranged from indifferent to opposed. I was a Paul Simon partisan during the primary Walker won.

But Walker worked hard to bring in additional Democratic legislators and the 1974 election produced three promising senators: Bill Morris of Waukegan, Jerry Joyce of Reddick (near Kankakee), and Vince Demuzio of Carlinville.

When I say Vince was the last to join, I should admit that suspicion of our meetings was not confined to Chicago Democrats. The three new senators had their questions as well.

I met with Morris and Joyce in Chicago to explain what we were up to. For the life of me, I can't remember whether Vince was in that meeting or not. I think my conversation with him was in Springfield, which is why I recall him as the last of the three to join the fold.

That was the group known as the "Crazy Eight." The name was applied to us by a reporter after a comment by Sen. Bruce. When someone questioned our individual independence, Bruce said, "Those crazies are so independent, if you'd put them in a truck, it would drive off in eight different directions." The name stuck.

Some thought the title irreverent, but I loved it. It seemed to typify the freewheeling spirit of the group. We really were independent and it took some careful maneuvering and nightlong arguments on the few occasions we all agreed on a single course of action. But, once you got the eight committed to a strategy, it generally succeeded.

Out of all that came some real changes: elimination of proxy voting in Senate committees, liberalization of voting laws dealing with registration and voting hours, a fairer share of education money for downstate districts, a reduction in sales tax on food and medicine, and on through a list of which all of us are proud.

Perhaps the most important thing we did was refuse to take leadership's word on how to vote. We assigned each member of the group to a certain number of bills and we met constantly to trade information. That energy bred like study among other members and it caused a revolution in the way senators addressed bills. When I first went to Springfield, all the work was done by leadership and some key chairmen. When I left, almost everyone was involved.

None of that attracted media attention, but it made a change and that's what we set out to do: To make us and others in the body more responsible. We were all very different in background and views, but we came together on that overall ambition.

Chicago didn't know how to deal with us. They tried everything you can think of to bring us into line, but nothing worked. We would vote with either Democrats or Republicans when the issue demanded it; we often split down the middle.

After delaying an organizational vote for five weeks in early 1977, we came within 30 minutes of taking over the senate and forging a bi-partisan chamber. That was one of the most wrenching experiences of my life and the Crazy Eight's high-water mark — but that, too, is a story to be told elsewhere.

Vince was careful about joining the rest of us for a very good reason: he was probably the most astute politician in the group. He could see the advantages and disadvantages of hanging so far outside of leadership and then banging your way in without compromise.

But he was better at basic, down-home politics than the rest of us, even the exquisitely political Terry Bruce and Dawn Clark Netsch, the one who really knew it all. The proof of that assertion is his continuation in the senate until his untimely death this week; the last of us to leave that body.

In his 30-year career he ascended to chairmanship of the state central committee and spent most of his years in senate leadership positions. He had a canny blend of idealism and practicality that all of us envied.

Others came into the group and departed over the years; the "Crazy Eight" swelled to thirteen in number by the time I folded in 1980. That unique legislative body gently spiraled out of existence two years later, but its spirit remained intact until this week.

(25 May 1986)

Chicago Mayor Harold Washington came to town Friday to converse with area mayors and to help raise money for local voter registration drives later in the year. Democratic party faithful gathered for a luncheon at Velie's to hear Washington speak and to chip in for the cause.

I would like to tell you what happened during his visit but the deadline for this column came a few hours before the mayor arrived. So, instead, I pass along some personal observations about the man and an account of the last time we had lunch.

I first met Harold in 1977, just after he was elected to the Illinois Senate. He was, and is, an impressive person: powerfully built, intelligent and street smart. Although he was a freshman senator that year, he was elected spokesman for the Senate's Black Caucus by the four veteran members of that group. They were all able and experienced men, but Harold was special.

He steered the Black Caucus vote toward the downstate group of which I was a member and we came within a whisker of breaking Chicago's domination of the Senate. We became seatmates and friends and spent a lot of time in conversation: dissecting bills, arguing, gossiping and trading yarns.

He was a fascinating speaker, addicted to Congeries, a literary device involving the use of repetition. He was also an effective debater. I remember, in particular, his arguments on a proposed new criminal code.

There was a strong push in those days to "get tough on crime. " Gov. Jim Thompson was lobbying for a new crime category, "Class X," with more emphasis on the title than on substance.

George Sangmeister handled the bill in the Senate and argued its merits so forcefully that I rose in support of the measure, bowing to George's reasoning and the desire of the electorate for some kind of action. Then Harold got up and peeled away the rhetoric, demonstrating the bill's serious flaws and shortcomings. I have regretted the vote since. My vote was popular; Harold's was right.

Later, Harold left the Senate to run for Congress. I saw him afterward in Washington, where he seemed to have found a permanent niche. Then, young Daley decided to run against Jane Byrne in the Democratic primary for mayor of Chicago and it became obvious to anyone who could count that a black candidate might have a chance.

Leaders in the black community knew there was only one man who could command the kind of respect it would take to win, so they talked Harold into leaving Congress to make the run. I followed that campaign more closely than my own and was delighted when my seatmate became the first black mayor of Chicago.

After he had been in office for a year, I called for a luncheon appointment. We met in his office on the fourth floor of Chicago's City Hall, for years Mayor Daley's throne room. We talked happily about old times and old friends, until it was time to leave for lunch. Then, the mood changed.

A security man ushered us into the hall and moved us briskly toward a waiting elevator. On the crowded first floor, bodyguards convoyed us outside to a waiting car. Police were holding up traffic until we were under way.

It was my first brush with that kind of security and I asked Harold how he felt about it. He said it was the one thing about the office he disliked. I asked if he received threatening mail. He told me death threats came in every day.

I became acutely aware that we were seated alone at a corner table where large windows joined. The buildings across from us would make excellent perches for disaffected citizens. I was not surprised to learn that he took most of his meals at his desk.

Writing before the fact, I can't tell you what we said to each other on Friday, or even if we had the opportunity to converse. But I can pass along something he said at an earlier luncheon. I asked him which title he preferred: mayor, congressman, or senator. He laughed and reminded me of a fellow who tried to accost him as we were leaving city hall. The man stood at the edge of the security cordon and yelled, "Harold!" until the mayor moved over to shake his hand.

"When people call me mayor, it doesn't mean that much," he said, "but, when they call me Harold, it means they know me as a person and trust me. I may not always want to be mayor, but I always want to be Harold."

(14 March 1996)

This week I drove down to Springfield for some work and fun. The work had to do with financial support for WVIK's reading service for the blind. The fun part was what one wag referred to as a "fossil hunt."

Actually, it was a reunion of former Illinois state senators. The last time one of these meetings was held was back in 1979 when I was in my last term. There wasn't much of a turnout then, but this time the hall was packed.

(If anyone still thinks term limits are a real need, please note that, of 59 sitting senators, only nine are left from 16 years ago when I was last in the chamber: four Democrats and five Republicans. There are far more alumni than members today.

The turnover is even more pronounced in the House of Representatives. Yet, we keep hearing that term limits are needed to assure continuing change: a classic example of fantasy crowding out fact.)

Past and present senators met at noon in the senate chamber for the start of a regular session. After the opening prayer, the current body pledged allegiance to the flag, to the amazement of the old-timers. Most of us thought that subject was pretty well covered in the oath of office, but I guess we live in testifyin' times.

There is one radical change in the chamber. Gone were the huge bill books which contained copies of all pending legislation. These monsters were planted on each desk and grew to three feet in height during a busy session. They were updated every night by a swarm of senate aides.

Instead, there sits in front of each senator a portable computer, hooked up to the Legislative Information Service. Whenever a bill number is dialed up on the voting board, it automatically shows up on each senator's screen.

If you want your party's staff analysis of the proposed legislation, you can call that up, too. I am told that there is a security barrier which prevents one side from getting hold of the other's information, but we usually found ways to do that in paper-only days, so they should be able to concoct a way to do it electronically.

Of course, we assumed that you could also place bets on the new machines, but then we veterans are a skeptical lot.

Each of us was invited to step up to the podium to list our years of service and make a pointedly brief comment. Depending on the person and the statement, applause, shouts, or hoots followed.

The 36th District was represented by four men who have held the seat since 1972: Randy Thomas (2 years), Clarence Darrow (4 years), yours truly (8 years) and Denny Jacobs (10 years and counting).

That night, we met again for a banquet at the Sangamo, Springfield's exclusive dining club. The only time I ever got inside the place back in the seventies was as a guest or member of a free-spending commission. It's still an impressive and tony restaurant.

The food was great, the bar well-stocked, and the conversation non-stop. Members of the "Crazy Eight" sat together and we marvelled that this was the first time all of had been together in one room in almost 20 years.

Phil Rock, who had served as president of the senate for longer than anyone else (and as a leader in the Democratic team for almost all of his tenure) demanded that a picture be taken of the "Crazy *%$# Eight" which had caused the Chicago organization — and the Republicans — so much grief.

For the record, the Crazy Eight consisted of Terry Bruce of Olney, Ken Buzbee of Carbondale, Vince Demuzio of Carlinville, Vivian Hickey of Rockford, Jerry Joyce of Redick, Bill Morris of Waukegan, Dawn Clark Netsch of Chicago, and me.

Later on, others affiliated with the group for varying periods of time: George Sangmeister, Earlean Collins, Harold Washington, Jim Gitz, Gene Johns, Kenny Hall, and Richard Newhouse. The craziest thing about the group is that it was seldom merely eight in number.

Along with deceased senators Johns and Hall, we missed Harold Washington, that great and good man who sat next to me and went on to become mayor of Chicago. Along with regret at his passing, there remains a residue of anger.

If he had just listened to his doctor, he might well have been there with us, reliving the good and bad times, and continuing to explore ways to make this often cumbersome democracy work better.

After the basic Crazy Eight posed, all of us gathered for the biggest group photo I have ever been in: all the senators and ex-senators in attendance. I'll be surprised if you can make out half the faces.

Bill Harris, the first president of the senate (1973-74, when the Republicans had a one-vote majority) chatted with us about some of the fights and fun we had, but the talk soon turned to the civility we enjoyed in those days.

When Bill presided, he met with minority leader Cecil Partee every morning to discuss differences and agreements and how to handle them in session. The mutual respect they enjoyed grew each time they talked things through, even when they differed.

When Partee took over from Harris, those meetings continued.

Don't get me wrong: the politics of the chamber were tough and both Harris and Partee could wield the gavel with force when they thought it necessary, but the debate seldom got to the level of acrimony and, even on those rare occasions when it did, we moved quickly to restore our civil relationships.

I'm afraid the quality of debate has deteriorated all across the nation these days. Ideology is replacing rational discourse and a willingness to find common ground. What that produces is not merely a breach of good manners, but a fracturing of the democratic process.

Sitting in that room of men and women who have known the responsibility of legislation and sharing our delight in each other, one cannot but entertain the hope that gatherings like this will reinforce the good will which all deliberative bodies must embody if they are to serve something other than narrow, partisan interests.

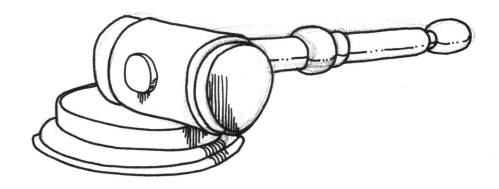

Television Follies

About twenty years of my life have been spent in television. That experience has provided me with a lot of subject material, from weathercasts to Kiddie Shows and the Commercial Planet.

(14 December 1986)

Cecil Partee, a distinguished black legislator from Chicago, had a favorite saying: "Everything that goes around, comes around."

That's a pithy way of saying that things even out, wins and losses balance, and you generally wind up where you started. Partee's First Law was very much on my mind this week as, for the fourth time, I returned to doing the weather on television.

Few people know it, but I started in television at WOC in Davenport, back in the fall of 1949, helping stage a weather program. I was a senior at St. Ambrose College and the only non-chiropractic student in the production crew.

My very first assignment was to help move the weather set in and out of the station's only studio, formerly the parlor of the old red-and-white farmhouse on Brady Street where WOC's modern plant stands.

I also helped shove the organ and piano back and forth from the parlor to the dining room for Marjorie Meinert and George Sontag, but the weather set was the first thing I laid my hands on. Little did I know that the contact was to mark me for life.

The set was actually a large stage for a marionette named Mr. Weatherwise, operated by another chiropractic student and voiced by a fellow named Pappas. The small, rotund figure waddled about the set, consulting papers in a miniature rolltop desk, looking out the window, pointing at dials, before finally announcing the forecast.

I didn't realize it at the time, but my fate in this world was to replace that dummy.

After graduating from Ambrose, I went to KWPC in Muscatine to learn radio, returning to the Quad-Cities in 1952 as a producer-announcer at WHBF-TV. Within a fairly short time I was asked to do the weather show.

That began a long flirtation with meteorology that kept me in the public eye for many years. I got to know the staff at the Weather Bureau and made some lifelong friends there. I was also drawn into the wonder of it all, amazed by the complexity of weather science and by its ambiguities.

I was especially fascinated by one of the fundamental units of weather, the thunderstorm, and read everything I could find about rapidly-developing theories of raindrop formation, shear, and funnel clouds.

I finally talked Les Johnson, manager of the WHBF stations, into buying a used, C-band radar unit from an airline and modifying it for land use. It was the first radar unit in the Quad-Cities, beating the local weather bureau by a few years.

With KEK-504 (or the Iron Eye, as I called it), I spent hours in my darkened office, watching thunderstorm cells grow and decay as they rumbled through the region. It was the oddest blend of tedium and excitement I have ever known.

But everything palls at last and I quit television and all its pomps to enter politics. When that aberration was concluded, WQAD-TV asked me to fill in as weatherman for a few months and I found myself back at the same old stand.

Not exactly the same. By now, everyone had access to radar as well as satellite pictures and reams of computer-generated information and graphics. It took this old dog a while to learn the new tricks, but it was still the weather and it was as absorbing as ever.

When that seven-month stint ended, I thought TV weather a closed chapter and concentrated on other diversions, principally public radio and a few eccentricities, such as this column.

But, once again, Channel 8 needed temporary help and, once again, I answered the bell. That's why, with gray hair, bifocals, and an uncertain air, I showed up on TV last night doing the weather. And will, I think, again tonight.

I still don't understand exactly why Fate has cast me in this role. It has permitted me other duties and honors, but I seem destined to spend at least a part of my life in front of a map, speculating about the movement of fronts and the possibility of precipitation.

Some folks disparage the calling. In fact, Chicago columnist, Mike Royko reserves his special scorn for TV weathermen and legislators, and I have been both. I often thanked God our paths had not crossed. When we met years later, he was merciful.

But those of us who practice the art, even as a sideline, know it to be an honorable profession with ancient roots. True, we now use computers instead of entrails, but we make our mistakes in public and accept the consequences.

That's more than the president can say.

(7 July 1996)

In a previous life, I worked in television at WHBF-TV in Rock Island. As far as the sales department was concerned, I was the weatherman. But, in my heart of hearts, I was Channel Four's Public Affairs Director and, as such, producer and host for "Spectrum" and "At Issue."

The latter program, a 90-minute discussion of controversial topics on Sunday nights, continued for some years after I left the station, but "Spectrum" was gone in a matter of weeks.

"Spectrum" came about when the CBS network vacated a half-hour slot at 9 p.m. on Tuesdays to allow local affiliates to produce their own public affairs programs. From 1960 through 1971, I got to spend a month researching a topic, finding an adequate TV focus for it, then presenting it live (in pre-video tape days) during that time period.

It was hard, but exhilarating, work. What made it so much fun was that Les Johnson, the station manager, gave me complete freedom to present subjects of my own choosing. I so enjoyed what I was doing that I never even thought of looking for a better job in the industry.

The range of topics was almost bizarre, from the first TV program on LSD to the origin of the Oedipus Rex legend. It was like pursuing a month-long course of study and then taking a test in public view.

Some topics took longer than others — I spent a nine-month gestation period before airing a biography of Sac Warrior Black Hawk — and some could be wrapped up in a week. But the one that arched over a several-year period resulted in four programs entitled "What's In a Name?"

Back in the fifties I became fascinated with the origin of names. There seemed to be a number of place names which made no sense or whose origins were lost to memory. So, I started compiling information and, when I had accumulated thirty minutes' worth, I put together a TV show.

After the first program, a young woman named Gail Brown started working as my secretary and researcher. She was a gifted writer (as Margaret Frazer, she currently authors a series of medieval murder mysteries) and a prodigious researcher. She prowled through libraries and wrote letters to post offices and local officials to pin down the source of as many local names as possible.

After I left WHBF-TV, they started cleaning out my files and many years of study went to the city dump. However, Pat Stout, who worked in the news department, managed to salvage some of the "name" files and presented them to me as a birthday present in the early eighties.

Just this week, I ran across those dark brown file folders, crammed with typing paper faded to a light orange, all of them criss-crossed with Gail's spidery, miniscule handwriting.

After spending a late night paging through her notes, I find that some names simply did not yield secrets. We know how Muscatine got its name, but no one can be sure just what the Indian word means. "Dweller in the prairie" is suggested, but it's just a guess.

Muscatine's problem in choosing a name was a fairly common experience: their first choice was already taken. Aledo was first known as DeSoto, but that name had already been assigned to another town. Determined to find a unique name, townspeople pulled letters out of a hat until they had enough to form a word.

Carrollport changed its name for a different reason. The Carroll family was very unpopular, so townspeople decided to choose a different one. Their first choice was Charles, but that name had already been assigned to a town in Lee County.

Looking for something unique, they settled on the Latin word for sand, "sabulum." One of the ladies present at that discussion opined that it would sound better ending in "a," so Sabula it became.

Some of the most interesting names resulted from English settlers attempting to pronounce earlier place names adopted by the French. Meredosia is a corruption of *"mer d'osier"* or "sea of willows."

I think the best examples of this are found in Arkansas. Low Freight has nothing to do with railroads or commerce; it's all that is left of *"l'eau froide"* — cold water. Smackover (often cited as a great "American" name) comes from *"chemin covert"* — covered bridge.

One of the great puzzles in American names was solved by a cartographer. In poring over old maps, he found the long-sought source of Oregon. It is derived from Wisconsin, but you would never have guessed it without seeing what happened on old maps of the upper midwest.

The French gave the name Ouisconsint to a river up north. The French sound, "wees-cohn-sahnt" produced the name Wisconsin. But on one map, the word was both misspelled and hyphenated. Reading the old map, you see "Ouaracon" (roughly "wahr-rah-cohn") on one line with "sint" below it. Thus, Oregon.

The problem with putting this kind of information on television was in finding a visual way of presenting it. Quite often, we wound up with me standing by a town sign explaining where the name came from. Not the most exciting TV, I agree, but the "name" shows proved to be very popular.

One of the most arresting stories concerns the naming of Quad-City towns; why Rock Island should be Davenport, why Davenport should be LeClaire, why Moline should be Rock Island, why Hampton should be Milan. It's been told too many times to be repeated here but, if you don't know it, it's worth looking up.

Gail's research didn't stop with names. Whenever she came across anything that looked interesting, she put it in the notes. As I looked through the pages, I came across a fair number of question marks and asides which I could not relate to anything.

But one sentence really stopped me cold. It was written in larger letters than usual and the ink was obviously applied with extra force. It simply asked, "What is the Ashtabula horror?"

Does it relate to the town name? A famous murder? A ghost story? "Spectrum" may be long off the air, but curiosity never dies.

What is the Ashtabula horror? If you know, drop me a line.

(27 August 2000)

No one is satisfied with the world he or she inhabits. So, we envision others.

For as long as humans have written, Utopias have figured in the literature: places and cultures in which a dissatisfied author imagines a life of peace and contentment, organized according to his personal taste. Whatever God had in mind in making this old earth, there are precious few humans who aren't eager to alter the divine blueprint.

It is, of course, an illusion. Total contentment for the thinking person is impossible. Even if the most exacting conditions of place, space, and the presence (or absence) of companionable people were arranged, sooner or later, every person capable of imagination would be dissatisfied.

It is the price we pay for self-awareness: the perception that, however ideal a situation might be, things could be a whole lot better than they are. It is a condition unique to *homo sapiens*. An animal doesn't worry about its life; it just lives it.

What compounds the difficulty for people is a lack of agreement as to just what constitutes a perfect world. One person's paradise is another's crashing bore.

Plato wrote of a Republic in which a happy life could be lived as long as poets were banned. On the other hand, Sophocles pitied the land in which "no poets sing." Sir Thomas More's Utopia depended on the rule of God, but such a rule must be administered by humans who can never quite agree just what God wants.

The quest for practical Utopias has produced a variety of communal groups, all of which have ultimately disbanded or modified their thinking and behavior sufficiently to persist in rapidly changing environments. Yet, even as such experiments fail, the search for perfection goes on.

For example, in our own time, a distinguished, creative thinker has conceived of yet another ideal world. I'm speaking, of course, of columnist Dave Barry, who has identified a Utopia he calls the Commercial Planet, glimpses of which are afforded us on popular television programs.

It's a place where cars are driven by stunningly beautiful people, but only on highways devoid of traffic; usually two-lane roads running along the Pacific coast. Or else the autos climb mountains like goats, or appear magically in remote locales.

On the Commercial Planet, pills banish headaches immediately; the pain of crippling arthritis evaporates with another over-the-counter medication; aspirin cures a heart attack; housewives laugh happily as they vacuum — or shampoo — their rugs.

In this media world mothers never fuss at kids or dogs which track in huge clumps of mud; that's because they have this magic mop that cleans with just a single swipe. Men with graying beards apply a bit of color and not only regain their youth; they suddenly learn to smile.

Life in this electronic civilization is so charged with possibility that serving a certain potato chip can send a party of munchers into a cross between religious ecstasy and orgiastic frenzy.

But even this Eden has its Dark Side. The Commercial Planet is also home to some people who are — how can one say this gracefully? — unbelievably stupid.

Just look at the folks who try to operate conventional (or Brand X) lawn mowers or weed whips: they are so uncoordinated that they cannot fill the gas tank without spillage or keep the whip from snarling. Watching their hapless attempts to perform simple tasks, one can only conclude that they lack a spinal linkage between brain and hand. Either that or they are in desperate need of a brand-new machine that can cut down small forests.

Then there's the poor guy whose auto air conditioner doesn't work and who solves the problem by filling his car with ice cubes up to his waist. And the woman who is fixated on laxatives and talks about them incessantly. She even purchases every brand in the store, bringing them home in order to read the contents of each to her husband.

I'm sure you can cite numerous examples of similar ineptitude and wrongheadedness. Fully half the people on the Commercial Planet are as dumb as the other half is suave, intelligent, and radiantly happy.

How can two such divergent types exist on one planet? Perhaps instant happiness and stupidity are somehow related: they might even be opposite sides of the same coin.

Or is the real truth of the Commercial Planet a message of redemption? Does this Utopia exist, not for the sake of its denizens, but as a beacon of hope for the benighted inhabitants of this one?

Call me a gullible tool of Madison Avenue, but I am convinced that these alien creatures, alternately foolish or brilliant, dejected or mirthful, are missionaries to the earth with a simple, but profound message.

The world cannot be changed in its entirety, but only in specific situations and in short, 30-second bursts of activity. No matter what problems darken our horizons: from kids who can't spell to irregularity, from the uncertainties of retirement to social rejection; there is a universal answer and the people on the Commercial Planet are doing their best to reveal it to an inattentive earth.

Got a problem? Change brands.

(10 March 2002)

Hard on the heels of Milt Boyd's obituary comes a new book from the University of Mississippi Press: "Hi There, Boys and Girls!" an overview of "America's Local Children's TV Programs" by Tim Hollis. Sure enough, there is Uncle Miltie on page 120 and, below him, a picture of Kay Duvejonck all duded up as as Princess Iowanna.

Mr. Hollis' scholarship in this area is impressive, but not infallible. He cited WHBF-TV's second kiddie show, "The Magic Carpet," as its first and brought to mind the effort it took to get that program on the air.

This was in the early days of Quad-City television. In the beginning, there were only two stations, WOC-TV and WHBF-TV, channels five and four (WOC-TV would shortly be moved to channel 6, where it remains).

There was constant and very real competition between the two operations. When WOC-TV announced the date for its first transmission, WHBF-TV went on the air shortly before — "for testing" — just to beat them. That happened again, years later, when channel five set the date for its first colorcast. Channel four, without fanfare, went first.

I worked for WOC-TV as a student in the fall of 1949. After two years learning the broadcast business at KWPC, the Muscatine AM radio station, I returned to the Quad-Cities in 1952 to take a job at WHBF-TV. (I wanted to work for a station that carried Ed Murrow.)

I was living in Rock Island during those Muscatine years, during which time I became involved with Playcrafters. During their 1951-52 season, I was cast as the villain in a melodrama. Along with many Playcrafter pioneers, there was an Augustana senior student in the cast named Jan Schrage.

I was bowled over by her performance skill and, when she turned up on the WHBF staff shortly after I did, I coaxed Forrest Cooke, the TV program director, to use her considerable talents in a children's show. I also wanted to get ahead of WOC-TV in kiddie programming.

That first show was only 15 minutes in length (quarter-hour programs were quite popular in those days) and called "Once Upon A Time." Jan sat behind a large toadstool podium and read stories, some of her own devising. Bruno Olson drew pictures to illustrate the tale and provide visual variety, and Jim Olesen or I provided extra voices. Either George Koplow or I directed.

Then we made the big move, renting some "Felix the Kat" and "Out of the Inkwell" cartoons, stretching the show to thirty minutes. Jim Olesen assumed the persona of Mr. Petersen, the Swedish Mailman, to add variety and help fill time. (In order to keep our limited supply of cartoons fresh, we ran only one or two each show.) We named it "The Magic Carpet."

Bennie Alter of WQUA radio was also into film and I hired him to do a double exposure of Jan and Jim riding a magic carpet, complete with steering wheel, through the clouds; falling to earth for the start of the show and riding away at its conclusion.

It was fun to watch — and sponsored, which made me a happy producer/director. But after only one season, Jan grew restive and decided to take the summer off to work at a YWCA summer camp for girls. I was stunned; leave television for summer camp?

That's when Milt Boyd stepped forward to suggest the character of Grandpa Happy. He took over the kiddie slot for the summer and, after Jan returned, made occasional appearances on her show.

When Jan decided to marry her college sweetheart, Phil Benson, and leave television for good, Milt took over the time segment and kept the show going for eight to ten years. Mr Petersen remained with the program and Milt's hand-puppet, the Ook-Ook bird, filled out the cast.

What I can't forget — no matter how hard I try — are those weeks when Milt was on vacation and someone had to stand in for him. Merciful time has erased the details, but I know that on several occasions, that job fell to me as Professor Litehead — Milt's idea, not mine.

I thought it curious that, while Jan went with her husband into consular service, Milt, Jim and I headed into education: Milt and Jim, full time; me, part time. I used to tell people we were trying to restore minds we might have damaged.

The Iowanna show was sponsor-driven. It was a Saturday morning program during which kids in the studio audience bid for articles using emblems ("Iowampum") taken from cartons of Iowanna products.

Milt was the auctioneer and the beautiful Kay Duvejonck served as the dairy's living symbol, Princess Iowanna. The program afforded her an opportunity to do more than TV pitches. She showed up everywhere the dairy ran commercials or promotions, including Channel Six.

Along with pictures of Milt and Kay in Hollis' book, you'll find details of early children's programming at local channels six and eight and at TV stations across the country. It's quite a catalog.

It also mentions some of the kiddie shows that were syndicated in the fifties. I wish the author had written more about the original "Time For Beany": Bob Clampett's 15-minute puppet show with the voices of Dawes Butler (Beany) and Stan Freberg (Cecil, the Sea-Sick Sea Serpent). When it came on, the whole production and engineering staff at WHBF-TV stopped to watch. Then, back to work on "Magic Carpet" and, later, "Grandpa Happy."

Now, Milt and Jim are gone; Jan lives elsewhere; Bruno, George, and I remain, well out of TV. But Hollis brings back those hectic, happy days in just a few pages.

Ed

These three columns are a touch repetitious, but each adds something to the story.

(21 February 1999)

The mid-point of the week was also its high point: Last Wednesday, I attended an Angerer Party, the first one in many months. It was an evening of understated elegance and thoroughly enjoyable.

I'm not sure how these soirees got started. Like the best social events, they began without plan; they just happened. I met Ed Angerer in the early sixties when I was hosting "Spectrum," a monthly, prime time show on WHBF-TV. I was on the lookout for interesting program material.

A friend suggested that I meet this young architect who had won some design awards that year, so I crossed the street to the Rock Island Bank Building and introduced myself. A few months later, we collaborated in a two-part program on church architecture: "House of God."

In later visits, I met some fascinating people: mostly architects who stopped by to pick Ed's brain about materials, one of his professional specialties. But there were others there as well: clients, builders, friends.

One night around 11 p.m., when I had finished up my TV chores, I noticed his office light was still on. I called and invited him over to my house. I usually took a couple of hours to wind down from my work and assumed that he could use the deceleration, too.

Without intending to, we soon established a pattern. I would put on a classical recording, each of us would prepare a drink (fine scotch for Ed, mixed with water and ice; vodka and orange juice for me), pick out a book or magazine, and start reading.

Two or three hours later, when the print began to blur, I would make one of those subtle suggestions for which I am famous: "Ed, go home." A few days later, we would repeat the routine.

It was after a year or so that I began to call these meetings Angerer Parties. A mutual friend, who occasionally joined us, gave our curiously unsocial events brief immortality in one of his short stories, transmuting them into what he called "Albanian Fiestas." In his reworking, each participant was given a bottle of vodka to drink in a room by himself.

After a while, we began to mix conversation into the readings and, in recent years, we have given up the books altogether.

Architecture creeps into the discussion from time to time. Ed can't help it; he is a person possessed by his profession. There is nothing else he could do or be. Architecture is his job, his hobby, his vacation. Even when he travels for fun, you can be sure he will find a building to critique.

I, on the other hand, have no fixed sense of profession. If there is a common thread linking the several parts of my checkered career, it might be teaching: everything I have done seems to have a magisterial aspect to it, from theatre and politics to writing and broadcasting.

I used to think that it was this contrast in profession which maintained the quiet friendship. But this week, we discussed a strong, common bond which may be the real key: we both work in litter.

My desk is always a mess. I have an idea where things are located, but a certain amount of burrowing is required to bring them to light. Frankly, I don't understand it. I am something of a neatness freak by nature, but you'd never guess it from my working environment.

Ed, too, functions in an office which looks like a warehouse. It is something of a shock to see those finely-detailed drawings and delicately-colored renderings taking shape amid a pile of boxes, books, and sections of shelving.

That was the topic we pondered this week: why is it that, in the performance of our work, we create and sustain such clutter?

At first, we tried to make a virtue of a fault, taking comfort in bumper sticker wisdom: "A clean desk is the sign of a sick mind," for example. But midnight philosophers must look for deeper meaning.

I reasoned that clutter is simply a byproduct of concentration. If you are working on a tight deadline — and both of us usually are — you tend to toss aside anything that is not essential to the task at hand. And, once tossed, there it remains until needed again.

Obviously, you could take time to tidy up, but the next deadline is already at hand, so your focus remains on what you are doing rather than on the setting in which it is done. So, over time, the stuff piles up.

Unfortunately, the discussion degenerated into personal attack: "My office is a lot cleaner than yours." In this era of relative virtue, it's okay to be disorganized, as long as the other guy is worse.

I argued from my memory of his office; he cited the paper glacier on my front porch desk. And so it went until the dog started begging for a trip outside. What we need is the objective judgment of a third party.

While not many will have the time or opportunity to check out both Ed's office and mine, there will be some whose needs and interests will bring them into our respective territories and it is to these few I address the question: which of us works in the most egregious white-collar landfill?

It won't be easy to settle the matter. In fact, I suspect that Ed might try to obstruct justice by doing some major housecleaning. But, having posed the question, there is only one honorable course of action open to me. As much as I'd like to straighten up my office, I really mustn't tamper with the evidence.

(14 June 1998)

Late Monday night, Ed Angerer stopped by to help me close out the day and start another. We did this often when I was working at WHBF-TV and he had his office at the Rock Island bank building: we'd both quit work about 11 p.m. and unwind at my home with conversation, music, and various portable.

Quite often, we'd simply sit and read until 2 a.m. Out of deference to Ed's age and professional standing, I was pleased to call these sessions — especially the silent ones — "Angerer parties." One of the sure signs of a decaying society is that we seldom have time these days to spend in such a civilized manner.

But this week, we reverted to happier times and spent the evening sampling iced tea, among other concoctions, while Ed sketched yet another approach to the stages he's been designing for me over the years. Ed is an architect as much by compulsion as by training, so it was only natural to start at the dining room table with pen and paper and arguments over the need for a proscenium arch.

Somewhere around midnight, we forgot about theatre and started talking about jazz. Ed is usually at his drafting table late Saturday nights when I am at the WVIK console sampling jazz albums we both enjoy. It was while chewing over some of these that we got to reminiscing about Al Barnes and the headliners he brought to the Horseshoe in downtown Rock Island over 40 years ago.

Ed was working summers at John Deere during those days and I had my first full time job after college at KWPC in Muscatine. We were not to meet for several years, but we were both spending as much time at the Horseshoe as we could manage.

I came with an old-fashioned wire recorder to get interviews with some of the performers, and what a roster it was! George Shearing's quintet, Nat Cole's trio, Nellie Lutcher, Louie Armstrong, the Mills Brothers, among others, each staying for a week. Rock Island had never seen anything like it.

I took Bernadette along with me (a very inexpensive way to show my fiancé a good time) for the first interview. It was with George Shearing who was one of the biggest names in the business that year. After the interview, he asked the two of us to stay until the next break and we wound up spending the whole night talking to him between sets.

He was in an especially good mood because his wife was going to join him at the end of the week. A young man named Dennis was serving as his valet (Shearing is blind) and he entertained us while George was performing. Between the two of them, we heard the most atrocious puns you can imagine, but it was a great time.

At the end of the evening, he asked us to return and we did. I have heard many in the music business complain that George Shearing is a very prickly customer, but he was a model of cordiality and fun during that week. He insisted over and over that Bernadette should have my radio job because her voice was so much better.

After Shearing, we spent time with Nat Cole and the Mills Brothers, but were unable to attend other shows. However, Ed went to all of them and recalls one night in particular.

It happened when Louie Armstrong was at the Horseshoe with Jack Teagarden, Arvell Shaw, and the rest of his small combo. One night Phil Harris and Rochester of the Jack Benny Show were appearing at Wharton Field House. When their show was over, they sped to the Horseshoe and crashed Louie's performance.

Ed maintains it was the swingingest, funniest night he has ever witnessed and, furthermore, some of it was recorded. He knew someone named, as he recalls, Phyllis, whose boyfriend was able to make some transcriptions. She lent them to him for two or three weeks so that he could relive the experience.

What, I wonder, ever became of those records? If you have a clue, drop me a line. It would be great to recreate those days when Rock Island was a premier stop on the jazz circuit.

The Horseshoe is now the Yankee Clipper and a long way from its glory days. The only visual reminder is the horseshoe in the pavement in front of 1608 2nd Ave., where Al Barnes' nightspot was located before he moved to the larger quarters across the street at 16th Street and 2nd Avenue. We jumped in my car and drove down to be sure the emblem was still in place.

I have always wondered what possessed Al Barnes to risk the kind of money it took to bring those jazz greats to town. Everyone speculated that he would lose his shirt in the venture, and I imagine that he did.

But money isn't everything, despite what the sensible people tell you. For many of us, Al Barnes was a hero, the man who, for a couple of seasons over 40 years ago, made summer evenings in Rock Island something special.

Ed and I spent an extra hour Tuesday morning saluting Al's courage, vision, and impeccable taste in music. Many people have enriched Rock Island with their energy and investments and to them we are grateful. But Al is special; he gave us memories.

(8 August 1999)

The news chased me all around the Quad-Cities this past Thursday without ever quite catching up. It wasn't until I came home at 4 p.m. that Bernadette told me what had happened.

Jim Loula had tried to reach me at WVIK, but I was in a recording session and it was the kind of news you don't leave in a message. He phoned again, just after I had left to begin a string of errands. Calls between the radio station and home finally came to cross purposes, with each assuming that I had, at last, been told: Ed Angerer is dead.

It was a body blow and I am grateful that it was delivered at home.

I have long read that you can never measure the full extent of a love until it is lost. That has been driven home to me several times in my life. Now that hard lesson is to be learned again.

The losses in my family circle have been mercifully few: my parents, two brothers-in-law, and, over sixty-five years ago, a brother I barely knew. But fate has been less sparing of my friends. Some of them I have talked about in this space; others, especially those separated by distance and time, remain in my thoughts, but out of the news.

But Ed occupied a special place, one that is hard to define. We met in the fifties and became lifelong friends. It wasn't just that he designed stages for the Genesius Guild or was able to sketch out plans for some of my crazier projects. We were simply and comfortably compatible.

Not long ago, I wrote of "Angerer Parties," the offhand name I chose for our occasional evenings of reading while listening to classical music and enjoying a libation. I have a large shelf of various brandies, bourbons, and other potables kept there just for his use.

They will gather dust now.

During our conversations I learned, to my surprise, that Ed and I were at St. Ambrose at the same time, but I was semi-cloistered in the seminary for the first two years. By the time I started circulating on campus, he had left for Iowa State and a life of architecture.

There are exceptional local talents in the field, but I always put Ed at the top of the list for the simplicity and clarity of his designs. He won prizes for them and served happily on the American Institute of Architects' Design Committee for many years.

I can point out several buildings in the Quad-Cities, from churches to a restaurant, that he designed and you can see his hand in them. We used to tease him about his fondness for straight lines and exact angles. Brother-in-law Loula used to say that was because they took his French curve away when he was a kid.

Back in the days when they published an annual listing of the area's most eligible bachelors, Ed always made the top ten. There were many beautiful women to be seen in his company, but none to be a life's companion.

I could go on and on, nattering in this aimless way, looking for the lightness that makes loss supportable. But the fact is that one of the principal points of reference in my life is gone. And I never recognized it as such until this day.

It's not as if we spent a lot of time in each other's company — in recent years, once every six weeks would be the average — but we were never more than a few blocks and a telephone call away.

But time has run out and the distance is now unimaginable. The amiable teasing, the fascinating discussions and arguments, the shared experiences — the Angerer Parties — are over.

Given another week, this column would never have been written. But the wake is today and the funeral is tomorrow and I have been asked to be a pall-bearer and to say a few words. I'm not sure I can handle it.

Ed was supposed to do those things for me.

He promised.

The Handy Man

My firm conviction is that Nature intended me for philosophical enquiry, solemn meditation, or some other sedentary profession. However sessile he may be, when a man presumes to buy a house and start a family, he can no longer avoid manual labor.

But I keep trying.

(28 December 1986)

One of the oldest traditions in religion is the keeping of a vigil in anticipation of a great feast. Thus, in Christianity, there is the pre-Christmas period of preparation known as Advent and the forty days leading up to Easter known as Lent.

These are usually times of deprivation and suffering, intended to cleanse the heart and mind and sharpen the joy of the feast itself. Some people regard these vigils as outmoded and artificial, but I think they spring from a basic human compulsion and, were they not already part of our Western heritage, they would be created anew.

What convinces me of this is the ritual we go through at my house just before any great feast. I should explain here that I am defining "great feast" as a visit from any or all of our children. These visits usually coincide with traditional holidays, but may occur at any time.

When word of an impending visitation is received, the penitential practice is decided. It always involves a 'Great Cleansing of the House' and is usually accompanied by some extraordinary sacrifice. This Christmas, when three siblings decided to spend the holidays with us, it was decreed that the attic should be cleaned; the floors sanded, stained and polished; and a major reordering of "all those papers lying about" should be accomplished.

And that's why I have been poking through layers of my life recently, trying to bring order to the past even as I continue to scatter and waste in the present.

I must report that the practice is a useful one: the floors are beautiful, the stuff in the attic piled in a different area, and the sorting of papers resulted in solving the Mystery of the Cuff Links.

I remembered having several sets of cuff links, but had not been able to turn them up for many months now. I was beginning to think I had abjured the wearing of ostentatious clothing and had given the cuff links to the poor in a fit of self-denial.

The answer turned out to be more prosaic. When, a few years back, we were facing an earlier visit from the kids, I had been asked to clean the closet shelf which I use as daily catch-all for the contents of my pockets. Apparently I was under some pressure of time on that occasion and had simply dumped the stuff into a box.

While shuffling through many such things last week, I came upon the box which contained, not only the missing cuff links, but a cross section of the things, people, and activities which occupied me in those days. It was like digging up a time capsule.

The great mass of material consisted of notes to return phone calls. I have a bad habit of writing down such obligations and then forgetting them. If the note surfaces, the call is made. If not; well, that's how I get into a lot of trouble. Judging from the quantity of notes in the box, I owe several apologies.

I also found a number of receipts which would have been useful at income tax time; a quantity of antacid tablets for which I still have use; one dollar and thirty-six cents in change; a small book on counting calories (its loss explains my body's altered outline); and approximately one pound of Kleenex.

Well, the kids are here and they and the house look great. And, I must admit, the preparation for their visit has been spiritually rewarding. It has given me a revealing look at my shortcomings and a strong motivation for self-improvement. In fact, my New Year's resolution is never to get so far behind in anything again.

And, my resolve is firm. What makes it so is the fact that I also found a gift certificate for five dollars worth of ice cream from Whitey's, a certificate which had expired.

(23 June 2002)

Last Tuesday, Bernadette decided to spend the day cleaning the second floor — all but the computer room, a space in which my junk and items of critical importance are so intermingled that it is not safe to wield a broom in there.

In typical husbandly fashion, I found that, much as I wanted to help, several pressing matters drew me from the house for the entire day. Just as well; the cleaning would not have been as thorough with my involvement.

After dinner, Bernadette brought down a handsome old wooden box which has been sitting in the main bedroom for many years. Each of us has dusted and relocated it from time to time, but I can't recall ever opening it.

That night, she pulled out a stack of papers, news clippings, letters, and pictures and started a journey backward in time. After hearing her exclaim over a couple of items, I joined her at the dining room table and there we sat until bedtime, rediscovering our past.

One four-page letter, written in pencil, was so old that it could not be deciphered. I took it to the office the next day and made enlarged copies in high contrast. It turned out to be a journal kept by one of her relatives traveling through Iowa in a horse-drawn wagon well over a century ago.

Along with complaints of mosquitoes, heavy rain, and hot weather, the diarist recorded such simple delights as wading in streams, drinking from a well of unusually sweet water, and encountering one kindness after another from people met during the journey.

The names were familiar to her: John and George, Ann and Wilma. But she could recall little else. I imagine we will soon be in for a round of long-distance conversations with her relatives out in Iowa.

There were other journals, mostly written by Bernadette during summer vacations. While she faithfully recorded our futile attempt to bring fiddler crabs and starfish back alive from Cape Hatteras, she omitted the mouse-ridden cabin we stayed in en route and the bug that flew into Steve's ear. Some events are so memorable, they require no written history.

I discovered that, during the better part of several years, she also kept a record of household expenses. Looking it over, I found it hard to believe that we stayed alive and well during the sixties on so little money. She would start with my generous $200, bi-weekly investment and start subtracting, mostly for groceries; which, I am happy to say, is still the major budget item.

December records were rather sketchy. She explained by noting that it was hard to keep track of everything during such a busy time. And, halfway through one fall month, she simply wrote "Impossible!" and stopped.

Tucked into the box, I found a brief genealogy that traced Bernadette's family back to the Mayflower. I had read in school how the bashful Miles Standish had sent John Alden to propose marriage to Priscilla Mullen and her celebrated reply: "Speak for yourself, John."

Little did I realize that I would wind up married to one of John and Priscilla's descendants.

Despite a niece's close study of the Wooten family, I remain largely ignorant of my antecedents. I am sure they were a fine bunch, but I don't think there's a Mayflower passenger anywhere along the line, so why bother?

Along with many newspaper clippings was one which has served me as an exercise in humility. It is one of the largest newspaper pictures I have seen — 14½ inches tall and 6½ inches wide — which appeared on the front page of the Quad-City Times.

It shows daughter Teri trying to get her kite out of a tree in Lindsay Park on a warm, windy day in March. I can't think of anything I might ever do to merit that kind of front-page coverage.

Bernadette also recorded Teri's earnest wish, many years earlier, to fly. After citing the impossibility of imitating birds, Bernadette finally suggested that she wish on a star. "How do you get on a star?" was her immediate response.

The next morning, Bernadette awoke to hear Teri leaping up and down on her bed (I assume she had figured out how the star-wishing business was handled), flapping her arms. When that didn't work, she dissolved in tears. I read that story now, mindful of Teri piloting airplanes today in Alaska.

David also kept a vacation journal, brief and to the point. According to his notes, the boys and I managed to watch Packer exhibition games while Chris, Teri, and Cece played on the beach at Wisconsin's Terry Andrae with their mother.

Digging through all this personal memorabilia, I came across a resume I once assembled for Bernadette. I have always maintained that she is the one who has served this community far more consistently and effectively than I and, several years ago, I decided to get it down in writing.

Looking at it now, I still find it hard to believe just how much she has managed to do while raising five kids: a charter board member of seven community agencies; pioneer work in Model Cities and agencies dealing with the elderly; scheduling entertainment for five Rock Island Summer Festivals and sewing costumes for the Genesius Guild. It's an impressively lengthy text, and it doesn't even cover her one-to-one dealings with people in need.

Did I mention that she also cleans house?

(15 May 1994)

Last Sunday I was settled in the hammock, contemplating clouds, when I heard a commotion behind me. Looking around, I saw a sizeable crowd forming in the street and assumed the worst.

My first thought was that I had been caught in the middle of a gang war, another innocent bystander trapped in one of those terminally stupid disagreements over the dumbest way to wear a hat or the transcendent value of one color over another.

A second glance revealed that the people were well-dressed, of all ages, and in an amiable mood. Several family groups were moving up and down the street and they were obviously looking for something.

It turned out that they had come to admire Mike and Jeannie's house across the way, one of several singled out for inspection in a tour of the Broadway District. (Broadway is the original name for 23rd Street. Its memory lingers in Broadway Presbyterian Church which caters to everyone, not just performers. But I digress.)

The Broadway District people had chosen Mother's Day for the event and it proved to be an excellent idea. It gave moms a chance to show the rest of their families how nice their own homes could look if certain people would just pick up after themselves and help around the house. A smart mom never passes up a opportunity like that.

Had I been a bit smarter and lot less lazy, I would have had my Weed Museum open for business that day. A ready-made crowd of sightseers like that doesn't come up our street that often and I had missed the chance to make a significant profit.

Oh, well; no point in hurrying now.

The next time around I ought to negotiate with the Broadway moguls about a tour of my house. It would offer a nice contrast to the stuff folks see at Mike and Jeannie's, for instance. There are precious few homes decorated in 20th Century American Accidental and I feel that a tour of my digs would gives moms even greater incentive for admonishing their families.

One personal benefit did accrue from the tour; it enabled me to put off for another week the Clearing of the Dungeon. An injunction for the prompt discharge of this assignment had been issued by the resident mom and it bore a definite finishing date, otherwise meals would be hard to come by afterward.

I dressed for the job (it pays to fake sincerity in these matters) and said I was ready to go to work, but she surely wouldn't want me to pile all that stuff in the yard while half the population of Rock Island was strolling by, taking in the sights.

She saw the logic of my argument and granted a week's reprieve. However, one can no more halt the calendar than the clock, so the time has rolled around and I am currently burrowing into the Dungeon in a spirited attempt to find the floor.

I call it a Dungeon because it's where various instruments of torture are stored. I am told it contains a lawn mower (more than one, actually; the first one ran out of gas), a weed trimmer, various implements for savaging trees and bushes, and God knows what else.

There is even a modern equivalent of the rack down there: a device which gained considerable popularity during the Inquisition and other periods of intense religious and political debate. It's called a Work Bench and I am told that, under its truly impressive accumulation of boxes and other material of less definite shape, one may find tools with which "repairs around the house" may be effected.

My memory of the wedding vows I took are, I admit, a bit hazy, but I really cannot recall a specific clause involving shelving. There must have been one: a solemn commitment, in sickness or in health, to fill every room with shelves. I say this because the subject comes up with some regularity, along with a reminder of my promise to put them up.

Once each new shelf is in place, I help fill it with things: books, records, souvenirs, socks, etc. An esthetic discussion usually follows which centers, not only on what ought to be put in drawers instead, but how acceptable shelf material should be organized for the most pleasing visual effect. I prefer the crowded look, but mine is always the minority opinion, so I wind up promising to build yet another shelf.

Of course, I promise a lot of things. It's a lot easier to promise work than to perform it. Besides, work in the future seems tolerable, even appealing. All one needs is a week's rest ahead of time, but even this minimal requirement is hard to manage. If for no other reason, I must get out of bed three times a day for meals, so I never have a chance to store up seven full days' worth of energy.

It's rather like trying to use a half-charged battery for full-power operations; even the Energizer Bunny couldn't get far in such condition. I'm sure lack of rest or some fundamental principle of physiology can explain both my reluctance to start these projects and my inability to get them done on time.

However, whatever motivation or energy I lack is supplied by my supervisor, so I am deep in the Dungeon today, sorting, rearranging, and disposing. It's steady, heavy-breathing work but it's not entirely mindless. Philosophical propositions are continually prompted as each new layer is revealed.

For instance: where did all these animals cages come from and what kind of shelf should I build for their safe (and tasteful) storage?

Now, That's Funny!

You be the judge ...

(6 August 1995)

A recurring nightmare became a reality this past week: after a late night at the computer, I fell into bed without setting my alarm. So it was that the telephone rang at 9 a.m. on Wednesday and a person politely asked my wife if I chanced to be at home.

Upon inquiry, Bernadette discovered that the caller was one of some seventy people who were gathered at Trinity Lutheran Church in Moline to hear me speak at that very hour.

Twenty minutes later, fully clothed, but unshaven, I stood at the podium in the church basement and delivered a rueful apology and a 60-minute discourse on a variety of things. The audience was attentive, responsive, and, thankfully, most forgiving.

I suppose if I were on the speaking schedule I used to keep, this kind of embarrassment might not have occurred. During my Halcyon days as Channel Four weatherman, I was invited to give several talks a week. Since talking is easy for me (shutting up, conversely, is frequently impossible), I was always happy to oblige.

But in those invitations, there was often included a phrase that would send a chill down my back and fill me with apprehension for days prior to the event: "Say something funny."

Only those who have never tried it can imagine that comedy is easy. Sure, funny things occur to a person in conversation and two *bon mots* in succession will earn you a reputation as a humorist. But producing the stuff on demand is a deadly business. I am never surprised to discover that celebrated wits are often morose and uncommunicative in private life.

What brings this to mind — and what occasioned the late night at the computer — is the annual obligation to update a comedy by Aristophanes to conclude the Genesius Guild's summer season of plays. It's a necessary function because the originals, after some 25 centuries, are well and truly dated.

Aristophanes lived in an Athens of moderate size: a town in which everyone knew everyone else. Thus, for example, he had only to mention Kleisthenes' name and the audience would roar with laughter. Mention the outrageous Athenian today and you must add an explanatory footnote.

So, my job is to turn Kleisthenes and others of his day into equivalent, well-known, contemporary personages and to stretch the plot far enough to strike a spark of recognition. But it's got to be more than recognizable and comprehensible; it's got to be funny.

In order to shorten the torture, I give myself just three or four days in which to complete the script and seven days in which to rehearse the play. Even so, the stuff gets stale in a hurry and, by the time dress rehearsal rolls around, you can't buy a laugh from cast or crew.

So, that first night audience decides for you, and only then can you breathe a sigh of relief or step behind one of those large, Lincoln Park trees to let your veins.

My inspiration is actually a kind of mantra which I recite before and during my brief stint at the typewriter: "I am going to write the funniest play ever written or they are coming to kill me." It doesn't produce masterpieces, but it does get me going.

In fact, this column is one of my last chores before turning to the comedy full tilt. By the time you read this, the play must be done. The first full rehearsal is this afternoon. I can make some corrections and additions through tomorrow night, but that's about the limit. Actors can get pretty testy if I push them further.

Weak or strong, funny or grim, the comedy is scheduled to open this coming Saturday night at 8 p.m. My version will not be the summation of lyric grace, obscenity, and slashing wit that Aristophanes originally concocted, but it will be in English, at least, and that may help.

I approach this task with reservations shared by others. Some years ago, I mentioned on the radio that I write the comedy each year and got a call from a man whose scorn was ill-concealed. "How can someone as square as you are write comedy?" he asked. Who knows? Maybe that's the biggest joke of all.

At any rate, in just six days, you can judge the results. Please keep in mind the dying words of actor Edmund Gwynn. In his final hours, he was visited by Jack Lemmon who asked him, bluntly, if it were hard to die.

Gwynn answered for everyone who has ever turned a hand to this business:

"Yes, it's hard, very hard. But not as hard as comedy."

(10 August 1997)

For the last ten days I have been in a sour mood. Not the best psychic situation to be in, I admit, but there's a very good reason for my dyspepsia: I have been working on a comedy.

It is a grim and bitter business. Most of us enjoy the finished product and have little occasion to question the process which produces our laughter. It's just as well; making comedy, like making sausage, is not a pretty sight.

If you think I overstate the case, consider what Red Skelton used to go through. Before his live performances, he would be violently ill. Only when he had settled into his act, gotten some solid laughs, and was sure that his routine was working, would his stomach stop churning.

You might laugh at the offhand way Rodney Dangerfield handles a heckler without knowing what excruciating preparation lay behind his polished retorts. Some of the most barbed comments he has to field come from a stooge, carefully rehearsed and planted in the crowd.

That man has to time his comments precisely — I mean, to the second — or Dangerfield will erupt like a volcano after the show. Timing is everything in comedy and the most casual, throw-away lines are usually the most carefully prepared. Dangerfield is a maniac about timing.

Of course, there are rare improvisational comics. Jonathan Winters and Robin Williams, to cite the two best-known of this type, can play off almost any situation and riff for hours. But they are not your normal citizens.

You really have to be crazy to be a consistently successful, impromptu comedian, and there's more than a hint of madness in both of them. Most improvisational comics work off a series of prepared routines, but must be satisfied with only sporadic laughs when they are truly winging it.

It also helps if your audience is slightly drunk.

But the very best comedy is the result of a discipline the Marine Corps would appreciate: meticulous preparation, constant rehearsal, and execution so polished and precise, it looks spontaneous.

This can be hard to explain to an audience — or to actors. The tendency in rehearsal is often to amuse each other, but that can be fatal. If you are entertaining each other, the odds are strong that you will not amuse your audience.

I often bore people with a story which illustrates this point. It happened when the late Bert Lahr — you probably remember him as the cowardly lion in "The Wizard of Oz," but his reputation was built during many years in vaudeville and on Broadway — was working in a revue and worrying about improving his act.

Although his routine was both funny and successful, he kept fretting about one detail that he considered weak. Finally, a solution occurred to him and he asked some of the other performers if they would mind staying after the show to watch — and judge — the alteration he wanted to make.

When the performance was over, a number of the cast changed into street clothes and, in a good mood, settled down to see what Lahr had in mind.

They chatted with each other and traded jokes while Lahr fussed about, setting up his props. Now, Bert Lahr is a naturally funny person and, as they watched him, they began to laugh at him as he encountered some difficulty getting things arranged properly.

His mood darkened as he fiddled with his props and, the more he fretted and muttered to himself, the more they laughed. Everything he did seemed hilarious. Finally, he completed his preparations and ran through the revised skit.

By now, they were falling out of their seats laughing, and Lahr's anger reached the boiling point: "Laugh if you want," he yelled, "but, dammit, that's funny!"

Ever the professional, Lahr wanted, not amusement for the moment among people he knew, but a device which would work with even the toughest audience. To get that, he needed precise, hard-eyed judgment, not easy laughter.

A true comic also understands the pain which undergirds his craft. Just think of those violent Tom and Jerry cartoons and how funny it is when the mouse plants a stick of dynamite in the cat's mouth. There's really nothing funny about it; except that it makes us laugh.

It's no wonder that some of our greatest comics relish black humor. Groucho Marx was once asked what makes a comedian laugh and he explained it this way:

"If you dress a stuntman like a little old lady, put him in a wheelchair, and have it roll down a steep hill toward a stone wall; everybody thinks that's funny. But, for a real comedian, it has to be a real little old lady."

A shocking statement, perhaps; but not surprising to anyone who works in the business. Just look at the familiar, paired masks of the muses which represent the theatre: Thalia (comedy) and Melpomene (tragedy).

Melpomene is depicted with a painful grimace. Thalia grins, but her smile looks forced, as if the corners of her mouth were pulled upward by force. It's not what you'd call an easy laugh.

But nobody ever said comedy was easy.

(8 August 1993)

Editor's note: During the first week of each August, columnist Don Wooten goes into hiding to rewrite a classic Greek comedy to be presented by the Genesius Guild. This year's play, "Plutus," 'is scheduled to open next weekend, so he is hard at work.

The play was written by Aristophanes and first staged in 388 B.C. According to Mr. Wooten, the original is "about as funny as leprosy," which accounts for his seclusion and desperate tone of voice on the telephone. During this period of time it is difficult to get a civil word out of him, much less a column. However, we found this poem taped to an arch door in Lincoln Park and think it will fill the space adequately. The author is this year's valedictorian at Rock Island Senior High and a member of the guild.

THE WOOTEN
By Emily Wood
(With apologies to Edgar Allen Poe)

Once upon a summer steamy, as I pondered, weak and dreamy,
Over many a quaint and curious drama that had gone before,

While I daydreamed, nearly slumb'ring, suddenly there came a
    grumbling,
As of someone softly mumbling, mumbling on the stage's floor:
"Tis some weatherman," I muttered, "mumbling on the stage's floor;
Only this and nothing more."

Ah, distinctly I remember, as each sweaty audience member
Braved the rain and muggy heat to listen to this ancient bore.
Eagerly I wished the morrow; vainly to escape my sorrow
As The Don his pride ingested to extract some precious ore:
Money from these loyal folks, with which to stuff the Guild cash drawer;
    Quoth the Wooten, "Help the "poor."

Then as God the heavens opened, sending rain, which't seemed had no
    end,
Soaking ev'ry plank of plywood to its very heart and core,
Foolishly we thought 'twas quite plain: none could act amid so much
    rain,
And we players tried to scurry home to 'scape celestial roar.
'Twas not so, we soon found out, as Wooten stood with mop before;
    Quoth the Wooten, "Dry the floor!"

Audiences often wonder if it's not a giant blunder
When Shakespearean garb looks like it's from the Army-Navy store;
With the ladies' frocks so ... stunning, and the gentlemen's tights all
    running,
And the chain mail, lovingly crocheted to help protect in war;
"Why can't we have decent clothes, like Music Guild?" we all implore.
    Quoth the Wooten, "Less is more."

And each year near season's ending, some Greek in his grave is bending,
As The Don revamps a classic comedy from Grecian lore.
While the chorus girls are dancing, and the chasing cast is prancing,
And even those with two left feet (like Bob) display their grace galore,
Someone asks, "Who's all this silly Fred-and-Ginger nonsense for?"
    Quoth the Wooten, "Terpsichore."

Then each year, as season closes, after leading us like Moses
Through the Greeks and Bard of Avon we might otherwise ignore,
Wooten ponders deep in his brain — is it really worth all this pain
To produce, direct, and act in near-forgotten works of yore?
Will he do't again, we wonder — suffer one more season's chore?
    Quoth the Wooten, "Nevermore."

At Season's End

After 50 years of pranking the park, my time with the Genesius Guild is over. But memories remain.

(18 August 1991)

Tuesday night in Lincoln Park.

Members of the Genesius Guild have just finished a line check for "The Acharnians," the full-throttle farce that closes out the season on Sunday at 8 p.m. It's the last line check of the summer. A full dress rehearsal on Friday, followed by two performances, and the 35th season is over.

It doesn't take long. The play only runs about 50 minutes and line checks wind up in half the time. It's my night for sentry duty, so I get a Pepsi and settle down on the bleachers to wait until the park closes.

Over at the band shell, the Starlight Concert series is into its last show of the summer. Rosie's Polka Dots have drawn some 500 people.

They fill the stationary benches and spread out in lawn chairs under the trees.

It's the kind of night you imagine for all summer evenings: temperatures are in the sixties; a soft breeze is blowing; the drought-thinned mosquitoes, no bother at all.

The music seems to come from another time. There is no overpowering, super-amplified beat. The lyrics are plain enough for the crowd to sing. Everybody seems to know "The Beer Barrel Polka."

Between the stage and the benches, couples dance. Waltzes are especially popular. Everyone seems to be smiling. Couples stroll away from the crowd, hand-in-hand. The contentment is almost palpable.

Two Sunday school classes from a Moline church are serving refreshments at the east shelter. It's worth a walk over and seventy-five cents for chocolate cake and ice cream. Quite a few are eating, but there is almost no litter. A gentle, civilized crowd.

Back in the bleachers, I lean back and check the sky. The Great Triangle is moving overhead. Vega, Deneb, and Altair: stars I first got to know on the roof of St. Thomas grade school in Memphis. They traveled up north with me and have been my companions every season on this hilltop.

Is it possible I have spent 35 summers in this park? I try to work out the time in my head. An average of (is it possible?) 30 hours a week for at least 12 weeks each season. That's 15 full days a year. Since 1957, close to a year-and-a-half out of my life, not counting time spent setting up and dismantling the stage.

And that's just the official time: the drama superintendent, Genesius Guild director shift. The fact is, I drift up here a lot when there is no obligation, just a desire to enjoy the quiet beauty of the place.

The soft glow of the park lights illuminates a scene that would be hard to fix in time. It must have looked this way 70 years ago when we imagine life was simpler, saner: the time of our grandparents who were wise enough to live life on reasonable terms, who knew everything, who framed the security in which we dwelt as children. Tonight, their world seems to have come alive again.

The concert ends with everybody singing "God Bless America." I join in at a distance, glad no one can hear me croaking along. The crowd streams through the park, heading in all directions.

I tour the grounds, lock up the restrooms, check that the roadway through the park is secure at both ends, remind some stragglers that the park is closed, and head for my car.

I stop at the corner and look back. God, I love this place! This is where my family and friends have idled, labored, laughed and argued as we struggled to "give to airy nothing a local habitation and a name." Was it merely theatre that we did? It seems so much more.

Driving away, I think again about my links to this plot of ground. I know it perhaps better than my own yard. It is as comfortable to me as my home. In a sense, it is also my home.

I have no idea what to expect after this life. Some of my friends assure me that I will gain an intimate acquaintance with fire, and they may be right. But if it chances that something of my spirit lingers on, it will not shuffle around my house, as much as I love the place.

I suspect my ghost will walk among the trees of Lincoln Park, listening to the music, admiring the stage, keeping vigil with the summer stars.

(28 August 1994)

Wednesday afternoon a diverse group began collecting in Lincoln Park to take down the Genesius Guild stage. It's an annual chore, usually undertaken on the Saturday following the last play, but this year we decided to get a jump on the schedule.

Two of us start at one p.m. and, by five, a total of eleven people are busy unbolting the metal frame, taking down the wooden facades, and clearing space in which to store this oversized erector set. By nine o'clock, the platform and towers will be safely stored for another winter.

As the oldest and most easily-fatigued member of the crew, I am permitted to take a few breaks, to sit and wheeze on a park bench and watch the others going about their work as diligently as if each were solely responsible for seeing the task to completion.

I wasn't completely idle, you understand. While awaiting a lungful of fresh air and a rush of renewed energy, I did some thinking. That's a major benefit of idleness: sometimes the mind will draw a rich meditation from whatever material is at hand.

As the crew worked to reduce the complicated structure to its smallest components, I reminded myself once again how much easier it is to tear down than to build up and how much more quickly the former task is performed.

It took us three weeks to get the basic units of the stage into shape and much longer to adapt it for each production. Now it was coming down in eight hours.

I got to thinking of how long and carefully we work at putting together what we value — a family, a community, a civilization — and how easily all such things can be put into jeopardy. One barbaric act can undermine a generation of civility and once the integrity of anything is broken, it is very hard to put it back just the way it was.

Yet, I reminded myself, life consists of this continual process of building up and tearing down. If we try to keep things as they are, there would be little potential for growth, for creative change. And the life-enhancing changes — leaving home to attend school, starting our own family, trying a completely new career in middle age — often require something akin to stepping onto a newly-built stage.

The three high school girls in the crew are looking for something else to do. Watching them cheerfully undertake another dirty and tedious task, I marvel again at their willingness to do whatever they are assigned. My thoughts roll back thirty years to a story guild members tell from time to time.

We were bringing our travelling stage back from Kewanee, after a very successful performance of "Othello," when two of the four tires on the trailer blew out, stranding us near Geneseo. Someone had to stay with the vehicle overnight and when that fact was brought up, one of the actors replied promptly, "It's not my stage."

Of course, he stayed. He took responsibility for that stage, even as today's workers are assuming responsibility for this one. How does it happen that some people are willing to assume responsibility and others aren't? Why do some run away from it and others seem drawn to it?

People often speak of the Genesius Guild as if it were my responsibility; something I did on my own. But, I promise you, there would be nothing to see on weekends if it depended solely on me or on any one person. The guild is an assortment of individuals whose collective efforts produce the stage, the plays, the fun. And that gang could do very little without the Rock Island Park Board, the Illinois Arts Council, local foundations, and a steady audience.

It is true, I started the group back in 1956 and have kept jealous watch over it ever since. But like the aging lover of an eternally youthful mistress, I know that, sooner or later, I must yield my place to another more promising and energetic suitor.

That's not a pleasant thought, but the truth is not always pleasant; it is simply true. My timeouts on the bench will lengthen until I no longer rise to take my turn with the work crew. As it is, I spend a lot more time pointing to work than actually doing it, so I guess the time is getting close.

It's also getting dark. I drag out a work light as we get down to the heavy lifting. Everyone is tired. One stalwart has to be up for work at the arsenal at six a.m. Everyone else has to turn out for work or school the next day, so we pick up the pace. I point more vigorously.

Afterward, those who don't have to get up early repair to the Village Inn for food and conversation. Several are planning to try out for an e.t.c. play coming up in the fall. They have not been worn down by the evening, but energized. Having wrapped up one season, they are eager for another.

I join in the chatter, but my thoughts start to wander again. I have this column to write ...

Of Ghosts and Time

(29 October 1989)

With Halloween in prospect, this seems an appropriate time to tell my ghost story. It may not be "real," but it is certainly true.

It happened in Memphis, Tennessee, on Marksman, a block-long street which contained about 18 houses, one of which was ours: a five-room home built on a simple plan. As you entered the house from a shallow front porch, you encountered the living room; after it, the dining room and then the kitchen. Parallel to those rooms and just to the left were my sisters' bedroom, my parents' bedroom, a bath and short hallway, and the back porch.

You'll notice that there was no room designated for yours truly. In the winter, I slept on a roll¬away bed in the dining room. On very hot summer days, I relocated to the back porch.

I'm not sure precisely when it happened, but I think I must have been in the sixth grade. I know it was in the spring, because I was still bunking in the dining room. And it was during one of those spring nights that I first heard the footsteps.

They were measured, unhurried, firm, and, I judged, masculine. They started in my sisters' bedroom, proceeded through my parents' room, made the sharp right-hand turn through the hallway into the dining room, came around the dining room table and stopped next to my bed, just at my left shoulder.

After a pause, during which I tried a number of things (calling out to mom, turning on a flashlight, throwing a book over my shoulder, or, finally, just lying there in a cold sweat), they started all over again in my sisters' room.

And so it went, night after night, during that spring and into the early summer.

Thinking back to those days, I remember trying to figure it out. I was not about to tell anyone, lest they think I had gone around the bend. I knew it had to be a product of my imagination, but I wasn't sure what was triggering the sounds or how I could stop them.

And I never got used to it. No matter how familiar those footsteps became that season, they still scared the pants off me. I reasoned that I could defeat them by not retiring until totally exhausted, so that I would fall asleep immediately. And sometimes that worked. But they would be back the next night, following the same track, ending with a definite one-two stop at my bed. Well, nothing lasts forever, not even ghostly walkers. But I must say, the conclusion was a memorable one.

The way my bed was positioned, I could look past my feet into the kitchen and into the kitchen pantry. One balmy night, I woke up and sensed that something was wrong. A gentle breeze was blowing the dining room curtains over my body and obscuring something in the pantry.

As I raised my head to get a better look, the breeze stopped, the curtains fell back into the window frame, and I saw a luminous face in the pantry. It was grinning, but the smile was not friendly: rather like the Joker's in 'Batman'. I hoped I was still asleep, but knew that I was wide-awake and frozen with fear.

Then the face floated toward me, out of the pantry, through the kitchen door, right up to the foot of my bed. No footsteps; just the face. At that point, I junked my inhibitions and tried to yell. A strangled sound came out but nothing loud enough to alert the family to my predicament.

As I prepared to leap out of bed and run for my life, the breeze lifted the curtains again and the face was gone. I never saw it again and I never heard the footsteps again.

Since that time, I have read a lot about the things kids hear and see as they are growing up: imaginary playmates and disembodied voices which usually disappear by the age of six. Perhaps a part of my brain was a long time developing, or I was just over-stimulated (that was also the year I discovered opera and girls).

Whatever caused them, the footsteps and the face are imprinted in my memory and I sometimes listen and look on dark nights, wondering if they will materialize again. Probably not right away, but maybe soon.

My guess is that, as they were products of a developing mind, they may be reborn in a disintegrating one. Footsteps and face may still be lurking about my neural pathways, waiting for synapses to fail as I sink into my second childhood; waiting for an encore.

It's something to look forward to.

(5 April 1998)

It was a slow day in the sixth grade.

I was sitting near the back of the class (one of the advantages of having your last name start with W) in the far west row, next to one of the big windows that lined the room.

The teacher was going over stuff we had studied the day before and I was bored. I was wondering why I hadn't been tapped to serve the funeral mass which was due to start at 10 a.m. Lord knows they called me often enough for Msgr. Maurath's 6 a.m. service.

Normally, I wouldn't have minded being passed over because funerals in our Italian parish could be tough on a twelve-year-old kid. It was okay if you didn't have to make the trip to the cemetery. Only one or two of the four servers involved had to take that ride out and back.

You'd think that would be an even bigger deal, missing all that extra class time. But, as I said, this was an Italian parish and funerals could get very emotional.

It was bad enough accompanying the casket to the back of the church after service. At that point, the choir would sing the Latin verses about the angels welcoming the deceased into Paradise and it never failed to move me deeply. Just saying the words "In Paradisum" was enough to get me going.

But that paled in comparison to what happened at the cemetery. In those days, the priest said the graveside prayers, consoled the family, then attendants started lowering the casket into the ground.

At that point, it was wise to have a few strong men on hand to keep family members from throwing themselves on the coffin. When that happened, everyone started crying, some at the top of their voices. If a Latin hymn could stir me, you can imagine how emotionally involved I got in that kind of scene.

So, while I really wanted to get out of class, serving at a funeral wasn't the best way to do it. I guess you could say I had mixed feelings about the whole situation.

As I was mulling this over, I glanced out of the window and saw a sight which has stayed with me to this day. Old Mr. Kubaki (I have no idea how old he really was; to a twelve-year-old, everybody is old) was up in the St. Thomas Church bell tower, leaning out and looking down the street.

So that's how they did it, I thought. When you were in the sacristy, waiting for the funeral party to arrive, the big bell in the tower would start tolling slowly about five minutes before they entered the church. It wasn't a burning question for me, but I had wondered how they timed things out so precisely.

It was just another of Mr. Kubaki's jobs. He seemed to do everything around the parish properties: a one-man work crew. He mowed the lawns, fired the furnace, swept up the school, repaired anything that broke, rang the angelus, and was also the lookout for funerals.

What struck me that day was the image of that slender, wizened man, leaning forward like a gargoyle, peering down the street. I stared at him until he suddenly straightened up, walked over to the bell, took hold of the rope just below the clapper and started those slow, solemn strokes.

I hadn't read any of Poe's works at that point, but when I did, Mr. Kubaki came to mind. From that point on I regarded him with something approaching awe: he was a messenger of death.

Suddenly I was convinced that, when my time came, Mr Kubaki would be back in that bell tower, announcing my passing to the world with those measured sounds. I was twelve and couldn't imagine the world I inhabited ever changing.

But it did.

I paid my last visit to Memphis about four years ago. Knowing that I wouldn't be back, I went to the old neighborhood, driving down the same street the funeral procession took.

I knew Mr. Kubaki wouldn't be there; he had left this world some years ago. But I wasn't prepared for other losses.

The school I attended had vanished. A vacant lot is all that remains of the focal point of my youth. Our old house was still there on Marksman Street, but Mrs. Acerra's, which separated us from the school building, was abandoned, with a gaping hole in the roof, obviously the result of a fire.

I parked across the street and got out of the car. The convent was still in place, perhaps still inhabited, but not by a religious order. Next to it stood the deserted church, sheets of plywood covering what remained of the stained glass windows I used to stare at every morning.

But the greatest ruin was the church tower. The bell was gone; the roof of the tower had collapsed into the top level. It was a ruin without grandeur: a grotesque wreck. That was the saddest loss of all.

I got back in the car and drove away. I couldn't get the image of the ruined tower out of my mind. In my imagination, Mr. Kubaki leaned out to watch me go.

And started tolling the bell.

Christmas

Almost every year I write something about the Christmas season. The content has varied from liturgy to cartoons. In 1996, I put together a string of information which hung together nicely.

I quote:

(8 December 1996)

Christmas is a confusing time. Compact of opposites, it exalts and exhausts, provokes anticipation and dread, fuses the sacred and the profane.

Think about it. Try to balance the material with the spiritual and you find yourself tilting badly. You know it's a religious observance, yet you are swamped by the holiday's material aspects: buying presents, getting a tree, planning dinners, parties, visits, and trying to get cards out to all the "essential" people.

These days, the secular part of Christmas has just about overwhelmed the sacred. True, churches receive their annual visitors on Christmas Eve and on the day itself, but that comes with a rush at the very end.

If you think I'm overstating the case, answer this question: what day is today and what is its significance? If your answer has to do with shopping at the mall or the Bears game at noon, you're in the majority, but you're off the mark.

Don't feel bad about it; not many folks recognize this as the second Sunday in Advent, the penitential season which leads up to Christmas.

The four Sundays of Advent are a casualty of modern times. In simpler, church-centered days, the month preceding Christmas was regarded as a time of spiritual preparation. The idea was that you had to clean more than the house to prepare for the feast.

In some homes — especially those of recent European immigrants — the Advent wreath is a familiar part of the season. It is usually placed on a table or cabinet: a circle of green with four candles fixed to it. Three of them are purple and one pink, or some lighter shade.

If your family still observes this tradition, you know that today you light the second purple candle. You also relight the first one: the one directly opposite the pink one. Next week, the pink one is added. The lighter color symbolizes Gaudete Sunday, marking the midpoint of Advent.

The Gaudete candle takes its name from the Introit of the day's mass: just a hint of the fun that's to come.

The Advent season is just about as confused as everything else about the holiday. Shortly after the Christian Church first started observing Christmas in the middle of the Fourth Century, some decided that such an important feast ought to have a period of special preparation.

This would also help tone down the boisterous secular celebrations Christmas was intended to replace.

In 490, Bishop Perpetuus of Tours ordered that a fast should be observed on three days of every week between the Feast of St. Martin (November 11) until Christmas. Other countries followed France's lead, but most of them set their own starting time.

In Rome, where Christmas began, they didn't get around to establishing an Advent until the Sixth Century, but they didn't consider it a time for penance. They just started celebrating early.

It took two more centuries for France and Rome to agree on an Advent period, but they bickered until the Thirteenth Century as to its exact length and its penitential character.

The rules were pretty tough. One bishop's proclamation banned wine, ale, beer, meats, fats, cheese, and certain fish. Nor did the prohibitions stop there. In those days the faithful also had to forego weddings, amusements, travel for pleasure, and sex.

The regulations have loosened up considerably since then, but I don't think they were supposed to be ignored altogether, which seems to be the case today.

Please don't think that I am one of those square-toed Puritans who wants you to forego earthly joys to concentrate solely on spiritual values. (Even though it's not a bad way to live and it certainly is a lot less expensive.)

No, I accept that the secular feast was here long before Christmas was ever thought of. The Romans had been celebrating Saturnalia from their earliest days with gifts, feasts, dances, and some excessively wild parties.

In fact, all across Europe and in many other lands, midwinter was observed as a time of peace, joy, and gift-giving. Your trips to the mall — even the football games on TV — have ancient and honorable precedents.

But the Christmas story builds on those ancient notions, adding some powerful themes for those willing to accept them: divine incarnation, redemption, salvation.

And, I submit, you cannot escape them. They will intrude at odd moments, even when you're hustling to yet another place where you hope to find the present which has eluded you for weeks.

It may be the hundredth rendition of "Silent Night" over the loudspeakers, a crib put next to a barbie doll, a single candle glowing in a display window, a mother taking time to comfort a very tired child: something, somewhere will bring you back to the center.

It happens. Even if you've never set foot in a church, you are not proof against such intimations. So, when the emotion registers or the thought comes unbidden, give it room. After all, it's Advent. A shadow of what it once was, I admit, but still a time to reflect, to prepare, and, finally, to accept Christmas.

(15 December 1996)

If you've been out shopping, you've probably heard more Christmas songs than you can stand. If you are a salesclerk, you'll likely be ready to cut Rudolph the Red-Nosed Reindeer's throat before he takes off on Christmas Eve.

That's really too bad because some exquisitely beautiful music has been written for the Christmas season, from Gregorian Chant to the modern carols of Alfred Burt. But the constant repetition of Christmas music as a merchandising tool can turn even "Silent Night" into torture.

If you spend much time in a shopping mall, you can probably tell exactly when the next rendition of Nat Cole's "The Christmas Song" is coming up. The best defense is somehow to block all of it out, then find a time when you can listen attentively, at peace, staring at the Christmas tree.

Notice I haven't used the word "carol" and that's for a very good reason. Not all Christmas songs are carols. There are two kinds of music composed for religious holidays: hymns and carols. Hymns tend to be pretty solemn while carols are simple and rather playful.

The first Christmas hymns were written in the 4th Century, just after the feast of Christmas was established. For the next 800 years, hymns were it. Then, somewhere around the 12th or 13th Centuries, vernacular songs began to be created by ordinary folks and the carol was on its way.

It's important to note that carols have been composed for almost all religious feasts. Back when the Genesius Guild was doing "Murder In the Cathedral," a play about the martyrdom of St. Thomas Becket, we found far more carols than hymns on the subject.

Carols take their name from the Greek "choraulein," a combination of words for dance and playing the flute. Such dances date from very ancient days and were normally done in a circle. The music, if not the dances themselves, traveled easily from the Mediterranean to Northern Europe and thence to the New World.

You can see the distinction: hymns are sung at church services; carols are sung at parties. Of course, language changes. By now everyone understands all music of the season to be carols and carols confined solely to Christmas.

True Christmas carols fall into several categories. Nativity carols deal with the event itself and are reverent in tone; prayer carols are addressed directly to the Infant; shepherd carols describe or give voice to these legendary witnesses; lullaby and cradle-rocking carols are to lull the Infant to sleep; Mystery carols recount legends associated with Christmas.

Companion and dance carols are especially delightful (e.g. "Bring a Torch, Jeanette, Isabella" and "Tomorrow Is My Dancing Day") as are Noels, songs in which "Noel" is sung in refrain. There are even yodeling carols, confined, as you might expect, to the Austrian Alps.

If you'd like to hear some splendid Christmas hymns, a quartet of women known as the Anonymous 4 has released a CD of such music. It's entitled "A Star In the East." It's a program of Medieval Music from Hungary, but its Latin melodies would have been at home in any European Cathedral between the 12th and 16th Centuries.

The Anonymous 4 also have an earlier album in the record bins, "On Yoolis Night." It is another medieval collection, this one combining hymns and carols, a distinction that none but scholars would bother with. One of the selections, "I Saw a Swete, Semly Sight" is the earliest known English carol.

This is haunting, other-worldly music, sounds that remove one to another, earlier time (I am listening to it while composing this column). One might term it incense for the ear, for it is of a sweet and sacred character. Why on earth the Catholic Church ever dropped such treasure from its liturgy is beyond explanation or excuse.

If you have roughly an hour to spare and would like to enjoy a work that is both deeply affecting and exhilarating, look no further than Ralph (pronounced "Rafe") Vaughan Williams' "Hodie." Vaughan Williams wrote this in his eightieth year, but it sounds as if it came from his teens. It will certainly be played on WVIK, but you ought to have this one in your home.

There is also a work by a British composer named Hely-Hutchinson, "A Carol Symphony," which is an instrumental interweaving of familiar Christmas tunes. Arthur Honegger's "Christmas Cantata" is heavier fare, but richly rewarding. And, of course, Handel's "Messiah," which is more directly concerned with Easter than with Christmas, but is splendid, affecting music.

Among many classical creations for the Christmas season, none is more directly appealing than Gian Carlo Menotti's "Amahl and the Night Visitors." If at all possible, experience this masterpiece in a live performance. If you are content with sounds only, find the original, 1951 cast recording on Victor (or BMG or whatever the label is called now). It remains the best recorded version.

There are endless compilations of carols and popular Christmas music on the market and making choices among them is almost pointless. If the musicians involved are good, the music will not disappoint.

One of my favorites is "We Wish You A Merry Christmas" featuring John Williams and the Boston Pops, on the Philips label. What makes this collection special is cut number three: "A Christmas Greeting." This is an arrangement of carols composed by Alfred Burt.

Burt was a trumpeter who wrote music to fit little poems by his father, a minister. He sent them as Christmas cards to relatives and friends. They are beginning to circulate among standard works and will soon become standards themselves.

The point of all this is to urge you not to pass over this music or permit it to become routine. There is more Christmas music than you will ever have time to hear, but, however much of it you encounter, try really to hear it, away from the mall, away from office hallways.

Give it a chance. In the right setting, without distraction, you will find it, perhaps, the principal joy of the holiday season.

(22 December 1996)

If you've ever been on a bus trip with teenagers, you know that, sooner or later, they'll start singing "Ninety-Nine Bottles of Beer on the Wall." It's a simple tune, maddeningly repetitious, but it does pass the time.

The nearest analogy to this kind of song at Christmas time is "The Twelve Days of Christmas." It has the benefit of a better tune and takes much less time to finish. But, like the beer anthem, it does go on rather too long.

Come to that, the Twelve Days themselves seem a bit too long. I mean, do you observe any or all of them? Does your family have customs associated with each day? Why do we still sing of them if they mean nothing to us?

Let's get technical here. The twelve-day observance is an extension of the octave. Both in Christian and pre-Christian times, great feasts were observed on the actual day and again on the eighth day (octave means eight). Christmas was set apart by adding an extra half-octave, extending its season to a full twelve days.

Once Christmas and its season were established, saints were assigned to them and numerous observances, traditions, and superstitions grew up around them. So many, that we'll deal with only six of them today, saving the rest for next Sunday.

Dec. 26th: St. Stephen's Day. The first day honors St. Stephen, celebrated as the first Christian martyr. In olden days, this was the day on which the church alms-box was opened and its contents distributed to the poor. From this came "Boxing Day," a time to reward public and private service. In England, servants carried boxes with them in which tips and gratuities were to be deposited.

Not a bad day on which to remember mail carriers, newspaper deliverers, and other accommodating folk who are often overlooked.

St. Stephen's Day also has some odd animal practices associated with it: horse races in Germany and a curious English custom of killing birds. Small boys would kill a wren, then display its carcass to the neighbors, for which they received a gift of money or food. This probably harks back to ancient mid-winter ceremonies; perhaps a dim memory of the substitution of animal sacrifice for human sacrifice.

Dec. 27th: St. John's Day. The "beloved disciple" (by his own account) has the next place. His principal tradition involves wine. It is said that someone tried to poison him, but the saint downed the evil potion with no ill effects. There is even an old Roman liturgy involving the blessing of St. John's wine, or Johannesminne.

It's not something I take lightly. We are assured that wine consumed on St. John's Day will protect the imbiber from being struck by lightning throughout the coming year. I'll bet your insurance agent would endorse this practice.

Dec. 28th: Holy Innocents' Day or "Childermas." This day honors the children said to have been slain by King Herod in the Gospel of Matthew. The story is likely a fiction. Scholars who take it seriously have differed on the exact number of victims. Statisticians reckon the number to be no more than 15; eastern savants count 14,000.

Whatever the number, this became a day privileged for young members of the church establishment: choir boys, acolytes, and students. During one period, especially in England, the youngsters were allowed to elect their own bishop for this day. He officiated at services, gave the sermon, and his rule was taken quite seriously by the older clergy.

The whole tradition of the "boy bishop" got seriously out of hand and had to be suppressed by the church. It did not die easily.

I wouldn't bother to tell the kids about this one; they make too many decisions in the modern family as it is.

Dec. 29th: St. Thomas' Day. This observance has a solid historical basis: Archbishop Thomas Becket was murdered in Canterbury Cathedral on this date in 1170 by four friends of King Henry II. The king and prelate, former drinking buddies, had a lengthy, acrimonious row after Henry had Thomas invested as England's leading ecclesiastical authority. Becket's murder was the great scandal of the Middle Ages.

It was also a blessing in disguise for the Pope who was having trouble keeping King Henry's hands off the church's privileges and property. So, the cantankerous archbishop was quickly canonized and King Henry sentenced to do public penance. This prolonged church authority in England for another four hundred years. Until, in fact, the 16th Century, when Henry VIII stripped Thomas' shrine at Canterbury — Europe's leading pilgrimage site — and other churches of their riches to build England's navy.

A good day to read Chaucer's "Canterbury Tales."

Dec. 30th: Nothing in particular. Better save your strength because tomorrow is:

Dec. 31st: St. Sylvester's Day. Not what you were expecting, eh? Everyone knows this day as New Year's Eve, a time for intense secular celebration. The Christian Church has done what it can to tone things down, but nothing has really worked.

It did make a stab at assigning religious significance to the day by dedicating it to Pope Sylvester I. Sylvester's distinction was that he was Bishop of Rome when Constantine established Christianity as Rome's religion. December 31st was thus advertised as a day of religious freedom.

As it turned out, it was just the opposite. The emperor started meddling in church affairs and the early bishops let him run things. Once freed from persecution, the church turned its energies to stamping out heresies and other religions. Religious freedom was a one-way street.

New Year's Eve is one of those time-haunted periods, when humanity celebrates its universal birthday. In olden days, people would make loud noises at night to scare off evil spirits, keep fires going all night long, wear masks and disguises (so that evil spirits couldn't identify them), and generally carry on with great exuberance.

I imagine you've been to parties like that.

Among the many customs of this day, let me cite just one: "first-footing," a popular feature of Hogmanay (that's what they called it) in Scotland. The character of the coming year was determined by the first person to cross your threshold after midnight. If that first visitor were a blond man who had been born feet first, you could look forward to nothing but good luck. Anyone else reduced your chances and a brunette woman spelled disaster.

Practical Scots used to hire blond young men to knock at their doors just after midnight and refused to open to anyone else. Prudence dictates that you check your New Year's Eve guest list carefully.

And so we proceed to ...

(29 December 1996)

Jan. 1: Feast of the Circumcision; New Year's Day. Hardly anyone thinks of the religious observance which marks the 7th Day of Christmas. Matthew's gospel reports that Jesus was circumcised on the eighth day after his birth, so it seemed logical to celebrate the event on the octave of Christmas.

However, it took four centuries after Christmas was established for this feast to make it into the Roman liturgy. Even then, some church authorities were not too happy about it. After all, the Christian church had substituted the rite of baptism for circumcision, so why bring it up at all?

But the real problem was with the secular feast of New Year's or Kalends. It was a time of unrestrained partying, a celebration of the

Roman god Janus. Janus was honored in the first hour of every day, the first day of every month, and the first month of the year, which was named for him: January.

Put all that together and you can see why the Kalends of January was an excuse for what S. J. Perelman called "high carnival and strange purple sins." It was hard enough to convert Saturnalia to Christmas, but the excesses of the January Kalends gave church fathers a real problem.

Romans used to spend New Year's Day in non-stop reveling and dancing in the streets. Think midnight in Times Square extended for 24 hours or more and you can understand the church's distaste for the first day of January.

However, the pagan aspects of the day were brought under some control after the 8th Century and the religious observance took precedence. But they couldn't stop tinkering with the feast. It acquired significance as a time to honor the Virgin Mary and also the name of Jesus, since he was given his name at this time.

But, to be honest, a religious relevance for this day will come as a surprise to most people. For modern Americans, it is the day on which people recover from New Year's Eve celebrations and watch bowl games on TV.

Jan 2nd: The Holy Name. This feast was split off from Circumcision and assigned to the Sunday between Christmas and New Year's. When there is no such Sunday, the feast moves to this day.

Jan. 3rd-Jan. 5th: almost nothing. There are numerous saints whose observances occur during this period — Antherus, Caspar del Bufalo, Rigobert, Syncletica, Gerlac, Oringa — but few of note, and none with ties to the Christmas season.

There is, however, at least one who deserves mention. Jan. 5th is the feast of Simeon Stylites, a saint with a taste for painful penance. He is remembered for spending his days on top of a pillar, without protection from the elements, fasting and praying. Phyllis McGinley wrote a delightful poem about this saint which concludes with these lines:

> And why did Simeon sit like that.
> Without a garment, Without a hat,
> In a holy rage for The world to see?
> It puzzles the age, It puzzles me.
> It puzzled many a Desert Father.
> And I think it puzzled the Good Lord, rather.

Jan. 6th: Epiphany. This is the day on which the Magi are said to have visited the stable at Bethlehem. Thus, it is the most appropriate time to exchange Christmas gifts. In Pennsylvania and other parts of the country with Christian Orthodox worshippers, that is the tradition.

It is a custom you might consider importing for your own family. It makes perfect sense, both liturgically and financially. You can do your shopping during the after-Christmas sales and save a bundle.

Epiphany was first celebrated in the Third Century, about a hundred years before the Feast of Christmas was established. It started in Egypt and was a Christian replacement for an Egyptian festival of midwinter.

The Magi are depicted as three kings today, with specific names: Melchior, Caspar, and Balthasar. The term "magi" really means wise men or magicians, and probably referred to Zoroastrian astrologers. There is no reason to assume that there were three; the number varies considerably in different traditions.

In secular terms, Jan 6th is the date for Twelfth Night, the high point of the Christmas season in England. There are numerous traditions associated with the day, with major emphasis on plays, pantomimes, and parties.

One Twelfth Night custom shows up in several countries and on varying days: the Bean King. A cake was baked for the occasion in which a single bean — or raisin, or rice grain, or almond, depending on the locale — was placed. A young girl (traditionally named Phoebe) would cut the cake and pass around the pieces.

The person winding up with the bean became ruler of the feast, selected a consort, and the two enjoyed the service and honor of all the rest. Back before the Puritans shut down Christmas altogether, Twelfth Night was considered the happiest part of Christmas, a celebration which would never die.

When was the last time you attended a Twelfth Night party?

A few centuries ago, people were so reluctant to end the Twelve Days of Christmas that they were extended. In Elizabethan times, the celebration continued until Candlemas on February 2nd.

That's a bit too long, by any measure. We do have to get back to work sooner or later. But I submit that crowding Christmas into a 24-hour period is too confining. We really ought to consider reviving at least some part of these Twelve Day traditions.

Let's have a Twelfth Night dinner this year. I'll bring the bean.

Who Is This Guy?

Joseph Donald Wooten was born in Memphis, Tennessee, on March 16, 1929. As he claimed in an 8th grade biography, this depressed his parents. Others sympathized, and thus was born the Great Depression.

He attended St. Thomas Elementary School. (They called it Grade School in those days.) When he was in the seventh grade, St. Thomas started adding a high school, one year at a time. After his sophomore year, Memphis parochial high schools organized a Catholic High for Boys. Wooten spent his junior year there, doubling up courses so that he could go on to college.

Assured that he should become a priest, he agreed and was sent to St. Ambrose Seminary in Davenport, Iowa, by Bishop Adrian of Nashville. Two years later, he left the seminary, but remained at St. Ambrose College.

During his senior year, Wooten worked part time at the region's first television station, WOC-TV. Upon graduation (1950), he took a full time position at KWPC-AM in Muscatine, Iowa, with the expectation that he would have a chance to do everything from news and sports to DJ programs and continuity. In November of that year, he married Bernadette Polka of Rock Island, Illinois. They settled in Rock Island and he commuted to Muscatine.

Two years later, Wooten made the jump to television, landing a job at WHBF-TV in Rock Island, where he remained until the end of 1971. This was a hectic period, during which he did some teaching and writing, and founded a classical theatre group, the Genesius Guild, while working in TV and radio.

In 1972, Wooten ran for the Illinois Senate and served in that body for eight years. Casting about for an ethical means of supplementing his income, he talked Augustana College into upgrading their 10-watt student station, WVIK, into a full-power, NPR affiliate.

After three years of shuffling frequencies and raising funds, the station joined the Quad-City broadcast line-up at 90.1 FM (later, 90.3) in 1980. That same year, Wooten lost his bid for re-election and settled in at WVIK as general manager, where he remained until retiring in 2003.

He also started writing this weekly newspaper column in 1986.

About the Illustrator

Bill Hannan, born in Illinois, raised in Michigan and schooled in Germany, taught for 34 years at Black Hawk College. He is known for his work as a calligrapher, book arts practitioner and as an author/illustrator. he is a prize-winning artist who has worked for a number of well known clients and his art is found in many collections both nationally and internationally. Currently, his work with books is examining the potential of digital imaging techniques. For the last several years much of his energy has been directed to illustration for books. This will be his fifth book he has worked on.

He has produced television programs on art appreciation, art history, Egyptology and Native Americans, including "Looking for Black Hawk or Someone Like Him" on which he was the program producer and director. He wrote and produced, "I am a Man, You are Another," a play/pageant in three acts about Black Hawk.

Bill is more or less retired, his area of teaching was in art, television, computers, advertising and "other stuff" at Black Hawk College, Moline, Illinois.

"During this time I used humor as a guerrilla weapon to fool my students into thinking that they are being entertained when in reality they are being educated," he says.

When he retired in 1998, Bill was a professor of art and was given professor emeritus status from Black Hawk College.

He participated in the creation of "Naked Came the Plowman," a book compiled by Quad-City writers and artists. He also was the director of the Riverssance Festival of Fine Art in 1999 through 2002. In 2006 he was appointed "Witter-Collins" fellow by the Mississippi Valley Writer's Colony.